D1141430

EDMUND SPENSER

Selected Poems

BLOOMSBURY
* POETRY *
CLASSICS

This selection by Ian Hamilton
First published 1999

Copyright © 1999 by Bloomsbury Publishing Plc

Bloomsbury Publishing Plc, 38 Soho Square,
London W1V 5DF

A CIP catalogue record for this book
is available from the British Library

ISBN 0 7475 4602 9

10 9 8 7 6 5 4 3 2 1

Typeset in Great Britain by
Hewer Text Limited, Edinburgh
Printed in Great Britain by St Edmundsbury Press, Suffolk
Jacket design by Jeff Fisher

CONTENTS

From THE SHEPHEARDES CALENDAR

Eclogue 1 – January

ARGVMENT.

In this fyrst Æglogue Colin cloute a shepheardes boy complaineth him of his vnfortunate loue, being but newly (as semeth) enamoured of a countrie lasse called Rosalinde: *with which strong affection being very sore traueled, he compareth his careful case to the sadde season of the yeare, to the frostie ground, to the frosen trees, and to his owne winterbeaten flocke. And lastlye, fynding himselfe robbed of all former pleasaunce and delights, hee breaketh his Pipe in peeces and casteth him selfe to the ground.*

Colin Clovte.

A Shepheardes boye (no better doe him call) when
Winters wastful spight was almost spent,
All in a sunneshine day, as did befall,
Led forth his flock, that had bene long ypent.
So faynt they woxe, and feeble in the folde,
That now vnnethes their feete could them vphold.

All as the Sheepe, such was the shepheardes looke,
For pale and wanne he was, (alas the while,)
May seeme he lovd, or els some care he tooke:
Well couth he tune his pipe, and frame his stile.
Tho to a hill his faynting flocke he ledde,
And thus him playnd, the while his shepe there fedde.

7

Ye Gods of loue, that pitie louers payne,
(If any gods the paine of louers pitie:)
Looke from aboue, where you in ioyes remaine,
And bowe your eares vnto my dolefull dittie.
And *Pan* thou shepheardes God, that once didst loue,
Pitie the paines, that thou thy self didst proue.

Thou barrein ground, whome winters wrath hath
    wasted,
Art made a myrrhour, to behold my plight.
Whilome thy fresh spring flowrd, and after hasted
Thy sommer prowde with Daffadillies dight.
And now is come thy wynters stormy state,
Thy mantle mard, wherein thou maskedst late.

Such rage as winters, reigneth in my heart,
My life bloud friesing with vnkindly cold:
Such stormy stoures do breede my balefullsmart,
As if my yeare were wast, and woxen old.
And yet alas, but now my spring begonne,
And yet alas, yt is already donne.

You naked trees, whose shady leaues are lost,
Wherein the byrds were wont to build their bowre:
And now are clothd with mosse and hoary frost,
Instede of bloosmes, wherwith your buds did flowre:
I see your teares, that from your boughes doe raine,
Whose drops in drery ysicles remaine.

All so my lustfull leafe is drye and sere,
My timely buds with wayling all are wasted:
The blossome, which my braunch of youth did beare,
With breathed sighes is blowne away, and blasted
And from mine eyes the drizling teares descend,
As on your boughes the ysicles depend.

Thou feeble flocke, whose fleece is rough and rent,
Whose knees are weake through fast and euill fare:
Mayst witnesse well by thy ill gouernement,
Thy maysters mind is ouercome with care.
Thou weake, I wanne: thou leane, I quite forlorne:
With mourning pyne I, you with pyning mourne.

A thousand sithes I curse that carefull hower,
Wherein I longd the neighbour towne to see:
And eke tenne thousand sithes I blesse the stoure,
Wherein I sawe so fayre a sight, as shee.
Yet all for naught: such sight hath bred my bane.
Ah God, that loue should breede both ioy and payne.

It is not *Hobbinol*, wherefore I plaine,
Albee my loue he seeke with dayly suit:
His clownish gifts and curtsies I disdaine,
His kiddes, his cracknelles, and his early fruit.
Ah foolish *Hobbinol*, thy gyfts bene vayne:
Colin them giues to *Rosalind* againe.

I loue thilke lasse, (alas why doe I loue?)
And am forlorne, (alas why am I lorne?)
Shee deignes not my good will, but doth reproue,
And of my rurall musick holdeth scorne.
Shepheardes deuise she hateth as the snake,
And laughes the songes, that *Colin Clout* doth make.

Wherefore my pype, albee rude *Pan* thou please,
Yet for thou pleasest not, where most I would:
And thou vnlucky Muse, that wontst to ease
My musing mynd, yet canst not, when thou should:
Both pype and Muse, shall sore the while abye.
So broke his oaten pype, and downe dyd lye.

By that, the welked *Phœbus* gan availe,
His weary waine, and nowe the frosty *Night*
Her mantle black through heauen gan ouerhaile.
Which seene, the pensife boy halfe in despight
Arose, and homeward droue his sonned sheepe,
Whose hanging heads did seeme his carefull case to
    weepe.

Eclogue 2 – February

ARGVMENT

*This Æglogue is rather morall and generall, then bent to
any secrete or particular purpose. It specially conteyneth a
discourse of old age, in the persone of* Thenot *an olde
Shepheard, who for his crookednesse and vnlustinesse, is
scorned of* Cuddie *an vnhappy Heardmans boye. The
matter very well accordeth with the season of the moneth,
the yeare now drouping, and as it were, drawing to his last
age. For as in this time of yeare, so then in our bodies there
is a dry and withering cold, which congealeth the crudled
blood, and frieseth the wetherbeaten flesh, with stormes of
Fortune, and hoare frosts of Care. To which purpose the
olde man telleth a tale of the Oake and the Bryer, so liuely
and so feelingly, as if the thing were set forth in some
Picture before our eyes, more plainly could not appeare.*

Cvddie.   Thenot.

Ah for pittie, wil rancke Winters rage,
These bitter blasts neuer ginne tasswage?
The kene cold blowes through my beaten hyde,
All as I were through the body gryde.
My ragged rontes all shiver and shake,
As doen high Towers in an earthquake:
They wont in the wind wagge their wrigle tailes,
Perke as Peacock: but nowe it auales.

Thenot.

Lewdly complainest thou laesie ladde,
Of Winters wracke, for making thee sadde.
Must not the world wend in his commun course
From good to badd, and from badde to worse,
From worse vnto that is worst of all,
And then returne to his former fall?
Who will not suffer the stormy time,
Where will he liue tyll the lusty prime?
Selfe haue I worne out thrise threttie yeares,
Some in much ioy, many in many teares:
Yet neuer complained of cold nor heate,
Of Sommers flame, nor of Winters threat:
Ne euer was to Fortune foeman,
But gently tooke, that vngently came.
And euer my flocke was my chiefe care,
Winter or Sommer they mought well fare.

Cvddie.

No marueile *Thenot*, if thou can beare
Cherefully the Winters wrathfull cheare:
For Age and Winter accord full nie,
This chill, that cold, this crooked, that wrye.
And as the lowring Wether lookes downe,
So semest thou like good fryday to frowne.
But my flowring youth is foe to frost,
My shippe vnwont in stormes to be tost.

Thenot.

The soueraigne of seas he blames in vaine,
That once seabeate, will to sea againe.
So loytring liue you little heardgroomes,
Keeping your beastes in the budded broomes:
And when the shining sunne laugheth once,
You deemen, the Spring is come attonce.
Tho gynne you, fond flyes, the cold to scorne,
And crowing in pypes made of greene corne,
You thinken to be Lords of the yeare.
But eft, when ye count you freed from feare,
Comes the breme winter with chamfred browes,
Full of wrinckles and frostie furrowes:
Drerily shooting his stormy darte,
Which cruddles the blood, and pricks the harte.
Then is your carelesse corage accoied,
Your carefull heards with cold bene annoied.
Then paye you the price of your surquedrie,
With weeping, and wayling, and misery.

Cvddie.

Ah foolish old man, I scorne thy skill,
That wouldest me, my springing youngth to spil.
I deeme, thy braine emperished bee
Through rusty elde, that hath rotted thee:
Or sicker thy head veray tottie is,
So on thy corbe shoulder it leanes amisse.
Now thy selfe hast lost both lopp and topp,
Als my budding braunch thou wouldest cropp:

13

But were thy yeares greene, as now bene myne,
To other delights they would encline.
Tho wouldest thou learne to caroll of Loue,
And hery with hymnes thy lasses gloue.
Tho wouldest thou pype of *Phyllis* prayse:
But *Phyllis* is myne for many dayes:
I wonne her with a gyrdle of gelt,
Embost with buegle about the belt.
Such an one shepeheards woulde make fullfaine:
Such an one would make thee younge againe.

Thenot.

Thou art a fon, of thy loue to boste,
All that is lent to loue, wyll be lost.

Cvddie.

Seest, howe brag yond Bullocke beares,
So smirke, so smoothe, his pricked eares?
His hornes bene as broade, as Rainebowe bent,
His dewelap as lythe, as lasse of Kent.
See howe he venteth into the wynd.
Weenest of loue is not his mynd?
Seemeth thy flocke thy counsell can,
So lustlesse bene they, so weake so wan,
Clothed with cold, and hoary wyth frost.
Thy flocks father his corage hath lost:
Thy Ewes, that wont to haue blowen bags,
Like wailefull widdowes hangen their crags:
The rather Lambes bene starued with cold,
All for their Maister is lustlesse and old.

14

Thenot.

Cuddie, I wote thou kenst little good,
So vainely taduaunce thy headlesse hood.
For Youngth is a bubble blown vp with breath,
Whose witt is weakenesse, whose wage is death,
Whose way is wildernesse, whose ynne Penaunce.
And stoopegallaunt Age the hoste of Greeuaunce.
But shall I tel thee a tale of truth,
Which I cond of *Tityrus* in my youth,
Keeping his sheepe on the hils of Kent?

Cvddie.

To nought more *Thenot*, my mind is bent,
Then to heare nouells of his deuise:
They bene so well thewed, and so wise,
What euer that good old man bespake.

Thenot.

Many meete tales of youth did he make,
And some of loue, and some of cheualrie:
But none fitter then this to applie.
Now listen a while, and hearken the end.

There grewe an aged Tree on the greene,
A goodly Oake sometime had it bene,
With armes full strong and largely displayd,
But of their leaues they were disarayde:
The bodie bigge, and mightely pight,
Throughly rooted, and of wonderous hight:

15

Whilome had bene the King of the field,
And mochell mast to the husband did yielde,
And with his nuts larded many swine.
But now the gray mosse marred his rine,
His bared boughes were beaten with stormes,
His toppe was bald, and wasted with wormes,
His honor decayed, his braunches sere.

   Hard by his side grewe a bragging brere,
Which proudly thrust into Thelement,
And seemed to threat the Firmament.
Yt was embellisht with blossomes fayre,
And thereto aye wonned to repayre
The shepheardes daughters, to gather flowres,
To peinct their girlonds with his colowres.
And in his small bushes vsed to shrowde
The sweete Nightingale singing so lowde:
Which made this foolish Brere wexe so bold,
That on a time he cast him to scold,
And snebbe the good Oake, for he was old.

   Why standst there (quoth he) thou brutish blocke?
Nor for fruict, nor for shadowe serues thy stocke:
Seest, how fresh my flowers bene spredde,
Dyed in Lilly white, and Cremsin redde,
With Leaues engrained in lusty greene,
Colours meete to clothe a mayden Queene.
Thy wast bignes but combers the grownd,
And dirks the beauty of my blossomes rownd.
The mouldie mosse, which thee accloieth,
My Sinamon smell too much annoieth.

16

Wherefore soone I rede thee, hence remoue,
Least thou the price of my displeasure proue.
So spake this bold brere with great disdaine:
Little him answered the Oake againe,
But yielded, with shame and greefe adawed,
That of a weede he was ouercrawed.

Yt chaunced after vpon a day,
The Hus-bandman selfe to come that way,
Of custome for to seruewe his grownd,
And his trees of state in compasse rownd.
Him when the spitefull brere had espyed,
Causlesse complained, and lowdly cryed
Vnto his Lord, stirring vp sterne strife:
O my liege Lord, the God of my life,
Pleaseth you ponder your Suppliants plaint,
Caused of wrong, and cruell constraint,
Which I your poore Vassall dayly endure:
And but your goodnes the same recure,
Am like for desperate doole to dye,
Through felonous force of mine enemie.

Greatly aghast with this piteous plea,
Him rested the goodman on the lea,
And badde the Brere in his plaint proceede.
With painted words tho gan this proude weede,
(As most vsen Ambitious folke:)
His colowred crime with craft to cloke.

Ah my soueraigne, Lord of creatures all,
Thou placer of plants both humble and tall,

Was not I planted of thine owne hand,
To be the primrose of all thy land,
With flowring blossomes, to furnish the prime,
And scarlot berries in Sommer time?
How falls it then, that this faded Oake,
Whose bodie is sere, whose braunches broke,
Whose naked Armes stretch vnto the fyre,
Vnto such tyrannie doth aspire:
Hindering with his shade my louely light,
And robbing me of the swete sonnes sight?
So beate his old boughes my tender side,
That oft the bloud springeth from woundes wyde:
Vntimely my flowres forced to fall,
That bene the honor of your Coronall.
And oft he lets his cancker wormes light
Vpon my braunches, to worke me more spight:
And oft his hoarie locks downe doth cast,
Where with my fresh flowretts bene defast.
For this, and many more such outrage,
Crauing your goodlihead to aswage
The ranckorous rigour of his might,
Nought aske I, but onely to hold my right:
Submitting me to your good sufferance,
And praying to be garded from greeuance.

 To this the Oake cast him to replie
Well as he couth: but his enemie
Had kindled such coles of displeasure,
That the good man noulde stay his leasure,

18

But home him hasted with furious heate,
Encreasing his wrath with many a threate.
His harmefull Hatchet he hent in hand,
(Alas, that it so ready should stand)
And to the field alone he speedeth.
(Ay little helpe to harme there needeth)
Anger nould let him speake to the tree,
Enaunter his rage mought cooled bee:
But to the roote bent his sturdy stroke,
And made many wounds in the wast Oake
The Axes edge did oft turne againe,
As halfe vnwilling to cutte the graine:
Semed, the sencelesse yron dyd feare.
Or to wrong holy eld did forbeare.
For it had bene an auncient tree,
Sacred with many a mysteree,
And often crost with the priestes crewe,
And often halowed with holy water dewe.
But sike fancies weren foolerie,
And broughten this Oake to this miserye.
For nought mought they quitten him from decay:
For fiercely the good man at him did laye.
The blocke oft groned vnder the blow,
And sighed to see his neare ouerthrow.
In fine the steele had pierced his pitth,
Tho downe to the earth he fell forthwith:
His wonderous weight made the grounde to quake,
Thearth shronke vnder him, and seemed to shake.

There lyeth the Oake, pitied of none.

Now stands the Brere like a Lord alone,
Puffed vp with pryde and vaine pleasaunce:
But all this glee had no continuaunce.
For eftsones Winter gan to approche,
The blustring Boreas did encroche,
And beate vpon the solitarie Brere:
For nowe no succoure was seene him nere.
Now gan he repent his pryde to late:
For naked left and disconsolate,
The byting frost nipt his stalke dead,
The watrie wette weighed downe his head,
And heaped snowe burdned him so sore,
That nowe vpright he can stand no more:
And being downe, is trodde in the durt
Of cattell, and brouzed, and sorely hurt.
Such was thend of this Ambitious brere,
For scorning Eld

Cvddie.
Now I pray thee shepheard, tel it not forth:
Here is a long tale, and little worth.
So longe haue I listened to thy speche,
That graffed to the ground is my breche:
My hartblood is welnigh frorne I feele,
And my galage growne fast to my heele:
But little ease of thy lewd tale I tasted.
Hye thee home shepheard, the day is nigh wasted.

20

From THE SHEPHEARDES CALENDAR

Eclogue 4 – April

ARGVMENT.

This Æglogue is purposely intended to the honor and prayse of our most gracious souereigne, Queene Elizabeth. The speakers herein be Hobbinoll and Thenot, two shepheardes: the which Hobbinoll being before mentioned, greatly to haue loued Colin, is here set forth more largely, complayning him of that boyes great misaduenture in Loue, whereby his mynd was alienate and with drawen not onely from him, who moste loued him, but also from all former delightes and studies, aswell in pleasaunt pyping, as conning ryming and singing, and other his laudable exercises. Whereby he taketh occasion, for proofe of his more excellencie and skill in poetrie, to recorde a songe, which the sayd Colin sometime made in honor of her Maiestie, whom abruptely he termeth Elysa.

   Thenot.   Hobbinoll.

Tell me good Hobbinoll, what garres thee greete?
What? hath some Wolfe thy tender Lambes ytorne?
Or is thy Bagpype broke, that soundes so sweete?
Or art thou of thy loued lasse forlorne?

Or bene thine eyes attempred to the yeare,
Quenching the gasping furrowes thirst with rayne?
Like April shoure, so stremes the trickling teares
Adowne thy cheeke, to quenche thy thristye payne.

21

Hobbinoll.

Nor thys, nor that, so muche doeth make me mourne,
But for the ladde, whome long I lovd so deare,
Nowe loues a lasse, that all his loue doth scorne:
He plongd in payne, his tressed locks dooth teare.

Shepheardes delights he dooth them all forsweare,
Hys pleasaunt Pipe, whych made vs meriment,
He wylfully hath broke, and doth forbeare
His wonted songs, wherein he all outwent.

Thenot.

What is he for a Ladde, you so lament?
Ys loue such pinching payne to them, that proue?
And hath he skill to make so excellent,
Yet hath so little skill to brydle loue?

Hobbinoll.

Colin thou kenst, the Southerne shepheardes boye:
Him Loue hath wounded with a deadly darte.
Whilome on him was all my care and ioye,
Forcing with gyfts to winne his wanton heart.

But now from me hys madding mynd is starte,
And woes the Widdowes daughter of the glenne:
So nowe fayre *Rosalind* hath bredde hys smart,
So now his frend is chaunged for a frenne.

But if hys ditties bene so trimly dight,
I pray thee *Hobbinoll*, recorde some one:
The whiles our flockes doe graze about in sight,
And we close shrowded in thys shade alone.

Hobbinol.
Contented I: then will I singe his laye
Of fayre *Eliza*, Queene of shepheardes all:
Which once he made, as by a spring he laye,
And tuned it vnto the Waters fall.

Ye dayntye Nymphs, that in this blessed Brooke
  doe bathe your brest,
Forsake your watry bowres, and hether looke, at my
  request:
And eke you Virgins, that on *Parnasse* dwell,
Whence floweth *Helicon* the learned well,
  Helpe me to blaze
  Her worthy praise,
Which in her sexe doth all excell.

Of fayre *Elisa* be your siluer song,
  that blessed wight:
The flowre of Virgins, may shee florish long,
  In princely plight.
For shee is *Syrinx* daughter without spotte,
Which *Pan* the shepheards God of her begot:
  So sprong her grace

23

Of heauenly race,
No mortall blemishe may her blotte.

See, where she sits vpon the grassie greene,
   (O seemely sight)
Yclad in Scarlot like a mayden Queene,
   And Ermines white.
Vpon her head a Cremosin coronet,
With Damaske roses and Daffadillies set:
   Bayleaues betweene,
   And Primroses greene
Embellish the sweete Violet.

Tell me, haue ye seene her angelick face,
   Like *Phœbe* fayre?
Her heauenly haueour, her princely grace
   can you well compare?
The Redde rose medled with the White yfere,
In either cheeke depeincten liuely chere.
   Her modest eye,
   Her Maiestie,
Where haue you seene the like, but there?

I sawe *Phœbus* thrust out his golden hedde,
   vpon her to gaze:
But when he sawe, how broade her beames did
   spredde,
   it did him amaze.
He blusht to see another Sunne belowe,

Ne durst againe his fyrye face out showe:
   Let him, if he dare,
   His brightnesse compare
With hers, to haue the ouerthrowe.

Shewe thy selfe *Cynthia* with thy siluer rayes, and be
   not abasht:
When shee the beames of her beauty displayes,
   O how art thou dasht?
But I will not match her with *Latonaes* seede,
Such follie great sorow to *Niobe* did breede.
   Now she is a stone,
   And makes dayly mone,
Warning all other to take heede.

Pan may be proud, that euer he begot such a
   Bellibone,
And *Syrinx* reioyse, that euer was her lot
   to beare such an one.
Soone as my younglings cryen for the dam,
To her will I offer a milkwhite Lamb:
   Shee is my goddesse plaine,
   And I her shepherds swayne,
Albee forswonck and forswatt I am.

I see *Calliope* speede her to the place,
   where my Goddesse shines:
And after her the other Muses trace, with their
   Violines.

Bene they not Bay braunches, which they do beare,
All for *Elisa* in her hand to weare?
  So sweetely they play,
  And sing all the way,
That it a heauen is to heare.

Lo how finely the graces can it foote to the
  Instrument:
They dauncen deffly, and singen soote, in their
  meriment.
Wants not a fourth grace, to make the daunce euen?
Let that rowme to my Lady be yeuen:
  She shalbe a grace,
  To fyll the fourth place,
And reigne with the rest in heauen.

And whither rennes this beuie of Ladies bright,
  raunged in a rowe?
They bene all Ladyes of the lake behight, that vnto
  her goe.
Chloris, that is the chiefest Nymph of al,
Of Oliue braunches beares a Coronall:
  Oliues bene for peace,
  When wars doe surcease:
Such for a Princesse bene principall.

Ye shepheards daughters, that dwell on the greene,
  hye you there apace:

Let none come there, but that Virgins bene, to adorne
   her grace.
And when you come, whereas shee is in place,
See, that your rudenesse doe not you disgrace:
   Binde your fillets faste,
   And gird in your waste,
For more finesse, with a tawdrie lace.

Bring hether the Pincke and purple Cullambine,
   With Gelliflowres:
Bring Coronations, and Sops in wine,
   worne of Paramoures.
Strowe me the ground with Daffadowndillies,
And Cowslips, and Kingcups, and loued Lillies:
   The pretie Pawnce,
   And the Cheuisaunce,
Shall match with the fayre flowre Delice.

Now ryse vp *Elisa*, decked as thou art, in royall aray:
And now ye daintie Damsells may depart echeone her
   way,
I feare, I haue troubled your troupes to longe:
Let dame *Eliza* thanke you for her song.
   And if you come hether,
   When Damsines I gether,
I will part them all you among.

Thenot.

And was thilk same song of *Colins* owne making?
Ah foolish boy, that is with loue yblent:
Great pittie is, he be in such taking,
For naught caren, that bene so lewdly bent.

Hobbinol.

Sicker I hold him, for a greater fon,
That loues the thing, he cannot purchase.
But let vs homeward: for night draweth on.
And twincling starres the daylight hence chase.

FROM THE SHEPHEARDES CALENDAR

Eclogue 10 – October

ARGVMENT.

*In Cuddie is set out the perfecte paterne of a Poete, whiche
finding no maintenaunce of his state and studies,
complayneth of the contemple of Poetrie, and the causes
thereof: Specially hauing bene in all ages, and euen
amongst the most barbarous alwayes of singular accounpt
and honor, and being indede so worthy and commendable
an arte: or rather no arte, but a diuine gift and heauenly
instinct not to bee gotten by laboure and learning, but
adorned with both: and poured into the witte by a certaine
ἐνθουσιασμὸς. and celestiall inspiration, as the Author
hereof els where at large discourseth, in his booke called the
English Poete, which booke being lately come to my hands,
I mynde also by Gods grace upon further aduisement to
publish.*

Pierce.　　　　Cvddie.

Cvddie, for shame hold vp thy heauye head,
And let vs cast with what delight to chace,
And weary thys long lingring *Phœbus* race.
Whilome thou wont the shepheardes laddes to leade,
In rymes, in ridles, and in bydding base:
Now they in thee, and thou in sleepe art dead.

Cvddye.

Piers, I haue pyped erst so long with payne,
That all mine Oten reedes bene rent and wore:
And my poore Muse hath spent her spared store,
Yet little good hath got, and much lesse gayne.
Such pleasaunce makes the Grashopper so poore,
And ligge so layd, when Winter doth her straine.

The dapper ditties, that I wont deuise,
To feede youthes fancie, and the flocking fry,
Delighten much: what I the bett for thy?
They han the pleasure, I a sclender prise.
I beate the bush, the byrds to them doe flye
What good thereof to Cuddie can arise?

Pires.

Cuddie, the prayse is better, then the price,
The glory eke much greater then the gayne:
O what an honor is it, to restraine
The lust of lawlesse youth with good aduice:
Or pricke them forth with pleasaunce of thy vaine,
Whereto thou list their trayned willes entice.

Soone as thou gynst to sette thy notes in frame,
O how the rurall routes to thee doe cleaue:
Seemeth thou dost their soule of sence bereaue,
All as the shepheard, that did fetch his dame
From *Plutoes* balefull bowre withouten leaue:
His musicks might the hellish hound did tame.

Cvddie.

So praysen babes the Peacoks spotted traine,
And wondren at bright *Argus* blazing eye:
But who rewards him ere the more for thy?
Or feedes him once the fuller by a graine?
Sike prayse is smoke, that sheddeth in the skye,
Sike words bene wynd, and wasten soone in vayne.

Piers.

Abandon then the base and viler clowne,
Lyft up thy selfe out of the lowly dust:
And sing of bloody Mars, of wars, of giusts,
Turne thee to those, that weld the awful crowne.
To doubted Knights, whose woundlesse armour rusts,
And helmes vnbruzed wexen dayly browne.

There may thy Muse display her fluttryng wing,
And stretch herselfe at large from East to West:
Whither thou list in fayre *Elisa* rest,
Or if thee please in bigger notes to sing,
Aduaunce the worthy whome shee loueth best,
That first the white beare to the stake did bring.

And when the stubborne stroke of stronger stounds,
Has somewhat slackt the tenor of thy string:
Of loue and lustihead tho mayst thou sing,
And carrol lowde, and leade the Myllers rownde,
All were *Elisa* one of thilke same ring.
So mought our *Cuddies* name to Heauen sownde.

31

Cvddye.

Indeede the Romish *Tityrus*, I heare,
Through his *Mecœnas* left his Oaten reede,
Whereon he earst had taught his flocks to feede,
And laboured lands to yield the timely eare,
And eft did sing of warres and deadly drede,
So as the Heauens did quake his verse to here.

But ah *Mecœnas* is yclad in claye,
And great *Augustus* long ygoe is dead:
And all the worthies liggen wrapt in leade,
That matter made for Poets on to play:
For euer, who in derring doe were dreade,
The loftie verse of hem was loued aye.

But after vertue gan for age to stoupe,
And mighty manhode brought a bedde of ease.
The vaunting Poets found nought worth a pease,
To put in preace among the learned troupe.
Tho gan the streames of flowing wittes to cease,
And sonnebright honour pend in shamefull coupe.

And if that any buddes of Poesie,
Yet of the old stocke gan to shoote agayne:
Or it mens follies mote be forst to fayne,
And rolle with rest in rymes of rybaudyre:
Or as it sprong, it wither must agayne:
Tom Piper makes vs better melodie.

Piers.

O pierlesse Poesye, where is then thy place?
If nor in Princes pallace thou doe sitt:
(And yet is Princes pallace the most fitt)
Ne brest of baser birth doth thee embace.
Then make thee winges of thine aspyring wit,
And, whence thou camst, flye backe to heauen apace.

Cvddie.

Ah *Percy* it is all to weake and wanne,
So high to sore, and make so large a flight:
Her peeced pyneons bene not so in plight,
For *Colin* fittes such famous flight to scanne:
He, were he not with loue so ill bedight,
Would mount as high, and sing as soote as
    Swanne.

Pires.

Ah fon, for loue does teach him climbe so hie,
And lyftes him vp out of the loathsome myre:
Such immortall mirrhor, as he doth admire,
Would rayse ones mynd aboue the starry skie.
And cause a caytiue corage to aspire,
For lofty loue doth loath a lowly eye.

Cvddie.

All otherwise the state of Poet stands,
For lordly loue is such a Tyranne fell:

33

That where he rules, all power he doth expell.
The vaunted verse a vacant head demaundes,
Ne wont with crabbed care the Muses dwell:
Vnwisely weaues, that takes two webbes in hand.

Who euer casts to compasse weightye prise,
And thinks to throwe out thondring words of threate:
Let powre in lauish cups and thriftie bitts of meate,
For *Bacchus* fruite is frend to *Phœbus* wise.
And when with Wine the braine begins to sweate,
The nombers flowe as fast as spring doth ryse.

Thou kenst not *Percie* howe the ryme should rage.
O if my temples were distaind with wine,
And girt in girlonds of wild Yuie twine,
How I could reare the Muse on stately stage,
And teache her tread aloft in bus-kin fine,
With queint *Bellona* in her equipage.

But ah my corage cooles ere it be warme,
For thy, content vs in thys humble shade:
Where no such troublous tydes han vs assayde,
Here we our slender pipes may safely charme.

Pires.
And when my Gates shall han their bellies layd:
Cuddie shall haue a Kidde to store his farme.

34

From THE SHEPHEARDES CALENDAR

Eclogue 11 – November

ARGVMENT.

In this xi. Æglogue he bewayleth the death of some mayden
of greate bloud, whom he calleth Dido. The personage is
secrete, and to me altogether vnknowne, albe of him selfe I
often required the same. This Æglogue is made in imitation
of Marot his song, which he made upon the death of Loys
the frenche Queene. But farre passing his reache, and in
myne opinion all other the Eglogues of this booke.

Thenot.   Colin.

Colin my deare, when shall it please thee sing,
As thou were wont songs of some iouisaunce?
Thy Muse to long slombreth in sorrowing,
Lulled a sleepe through loues misgouernaunce.
Now somewhat sing, whose endles souenaunce,
Emong the shepeheards swaines may aye remaine,
Whether thee list thy loued lasse aduaunce,
Or honor *Pan* with hymnes of higher vaine.

Colin.

Thenot, now nis the time of merimake.
Nor *Pan* to herye, nor with loue to playe:
Sike myrth in May is meetest for to make,
Or summer shade vnder the cocked haye.

35

But nowe sadde Winter welked hath the day,
And *Phœbus* weary of his yerely taske,
Ystabled hath his steedes in lowlye laye,
And taken vp his ynne in *Fishes* haske.
Thilke sollein season sadder plight doth aske:
And loatheth sike delightes, as thou doest prayse:
The mornefull Muse in myrth now list ne maske,
As shee was wont in youngth and sommer dayes.
But if thou algate lust light virelayes,
And looser songs of loue to vnderfong
Who but thy selfe deserues sike Poetes prayse?
Relieue thy Oaten pypes, that sleepen long.

Thenot.

The Nightingale is souereigne of song,
Before him sits the Titmose silent bee:
And I vnfitte to thrust in skilfull thronge,
Should *Colin* make iudge of my fooleree.
Nay, better learne of hem, that learned bee,
And han be watered at the Muses well:
The kindlye dewe drops from the higher tree,
And wets the little plants that lowly dwell.
But if sadde winters wrathe and season chill,
Accorde not with thy Muses meriment:
To sadder times thou mayst attune thy quill,
And sing of sorrowe and deathes dreeriment.
For deade is Dido, dead alas and drent,
Dido the great shepehearde his daughter sheene:
The fayrest May she was that euer went,

36

Her like shee has not left behinde I weene.
And if thou wilt bewayle my wofull tene:
I shall thee giue yond Cosset for thy payne:
And if thy rymes as rownd and rufull bene,
As those that did thy *Rosalind* complayne,
Much greater gyfts for guerdon thou shalt gayne,
Then Kidde or Cosset, which I thee bynempt:
Then vp I say, thou iolly shepeheard swayne,
Let not my small demaund be so contempt.

Colin.

Thenot to that I choose, thou doest me tempt,
But ah to well I wote my humble vaine,
And howe my rymes bene rugged and vnkempt:
Yet as I conne, my conning I will strayne.

Vp then *Melpomene* thou mournefulst Muse of nyne,
Such cause of mourning neuer hadst afore:
Vp grieslie ghostes and vp my rufull ryme,
Matter of myrth now shalt thou haue no more.
For dead shee is, that myrth thee made of yore.
  Dido my deare alas is dead,
  Dead and lyeth wrapt in lead:
    O heauie herse,
Let streaming teares be poured out in store:
    O carefull verse.

Shepheards, that by your flocks on Kentish downes
  abyde,

Waile ye this wofull waste of natures warke:
Waile we the wight, whose presence was our pryde:
Waile we the wight, whose absence is our carke.
The sonne of all the world is dimme and darke:
    The earth now lacks her wonted light,
    And all we dwell in deadly night,
        O heauie herse.
Breake we our pypes, that shrild as lowde as Larke,
        O carefull verse.

Why doe we longer liue, (ah why liue we so long)
Whose better dayes death hath shut vp in woe?
The fayrest floure our gyrlond all emong,
Is faded quite and into dust ygoe.
Sing now ye shepheardes daughters, sing no moe
    The songs that *Colin* made in her prayse,
    But into weeping turne your wanton layes,
        O heauie herse,
Now is time to dye. Nay time was long ygoe,
        O carefull verse.

Whence is it, that the flouret of the field doth fade,
And lyeth buryed long in Winters bale:
Yet soone as spring his mantle doth display,
It floureth fresh, as it should neuer fayle?
But thing on earth that is of most availe,
    As vertues braunch and beauties budde,
    Reliuen not for any good.
        O heauie herse,

38

The braunch once dead, the budde eke needes must
   quaile,
     O carefull verse.

She while she was, (that was, a woful word to sayne)
For beauties prayse and plesaunce had no pere
So well she couth the shepherds entertayne,
With cakes and cracknells and such country chere.
Ne would she scorne the simple shepheards swaine,
   For she would cal hem often heme
   And giue hem curds and clouted Creame.
     O heauie herse,
Als *Colin cloute* she would not once disdayne.
     O carefull verse.

But nowe sike happy cheere is turnd to heauie
   chaunce,
Such pleasaunce now displast by dolors dint:
All Musick sleepes, where death doth leade the
   daunce,
And shepherds wonted solace is extinct.
The blew in black, the greene in gray is tinct,
   The gaudie girlonds deck her graue,
   The faded flowres her corse embraue.
     O heauie herse,
Morne nowe my Muse, now morne with teares
   besprint.
     O carefull verse.

O thou greate shepheard *Lobbin*, how great is thy
   griefe,
Where bene the nosegayes that she dight for thee:
The colourd chaplets wrought with a chiefe,
The knotted rushrings, and gilte Rosemaree?
For shee deemed nothing too deere for thee.
  Ah they bene all yclad in clay,
  One bitter blast blewe all away.
    O heauie herse,
Thereof nought remaynes but the memoree.
    O carefull verse.

Ay me that dreerie death should strike so mortall
   stroke,
That can vndoe Dame natures kindly course:
The faded lockes fall from the loftie oke,
The flouds do gaspe, for dryed is theyr sourse,
And flouds of teares flowe in theyr stead perforse.
  The mantled medowes mourne,
  Theyr sondry colours tourne.
    O heauie herse,
The heauens doe melt in teares without remorse.
    O carefull verse.

The feeble flocks in field refuse their former foode,
And hang theyr heads, as they would learne to weepe:
The beastes in forest wayle as they were woode,
Except the Wolues, that chase the wandring sheepe:
Now she is gon that safely did hem keepe,

The Turtle on the bared braunch,
Laments the wound, that death did launch.
    O heauie herse,
And *Philomele* her song with teares doth steepe.
    O carefull verse.

The water Nymphs, that wont with her to sing and
    daunce,
And for her girlond Oliue braunches beare,
Now balefull boughes of Cypres doen aduaunce:
The Muses, that were wont greene bayes to weare,
Now bringen bitter Eldre braunches seare,
    The fatall sisters eke repent,
    Her vitall threde so soone was spent.
        O heauie herse,
Morne now my Muse, now morne with heauie cheare.
    O carefull verse.

O trustlesse state of earthly things, and slipper hope
Of mortal men, that swincke and sweate for nought,
And shooting wide, doe misse the marked scope:
Now haue I learnd (a lesson derely bought)
That nys on earth assuraunce to be sought:
    For what might be in earthlie mould,
    That did her buried body hould,
        O heauie herse,
Yet saw I on the beare when it was brought
    O carefull verse.

But maugre death, and dreaded sisters deadly spight,
And gates of hel, and fyrie furies forse:
She hath the bonds broke of eternall night,
Her soule vnbodied of the burdenous corpse.
Why then weepes Lobbin so without remorse?
  O Lobb, thy losse no longer lament,
  Dido nis dead, but into heauen hent.
    O happye herse,
Cease now my Muse, now cease thy sorrowes sourse,
    O ioyfull verse.

Why wayle we then? why weary we the Gods with
    playnts,
As if some euill were to her betight?
She raignes a goddesse now emong the saintes,
That whilome was the saynt of shepheardes light:
And is enstalled nowe in heauens hight.
  I see thee blessed soule, I see,
  Walke in *Elisian* fieldes so free.
    O happy herse,
Might I once come to thee (O that I might)
    O ioyfull verse.

Vnwise and wretched men to weete whats good or ill,
We deeme of Death as doome of ill desert:
But knewe we fooles, what it vs bringes vntil,
Dye would we dayly, once it to expert.
No daunger there the shepheard can astert:
  Fayre fieldes and pleasaunt layes there bene,

42

The fieldes ay fresh, the grasse ay greene:
    O happy herse,
Make hast ye shepheards, thether to reuert,
    O ioyfull verse.

Dido is gone afore (whose turne shall be the next?)
There liues shee with the blessed Gods in blisse,
There drincks she *Nectar* with *Ambrosia* mixt,
And ioyes enioyes, that mortall men doe misse.
The honor now of highest gods she is,
    The whilome was poore shepheards pryde,
    While here on earth she did abyde.
        O happy herse,
Ceasse now my song, my woe now wasted is.
        O ioyfull verse.

                    Thenot.
Ay francke shepheard, how bene thy verses meint
With doolful pleasaunce, so as I ne wotte,
Whether reioyce or weepe for great constrainte?
Thyne be the cossette, well hast thow it gotte.
Vp *Colin* vp, ynough thou morned hast,
Now gynnes to mizzle, hye we homeward fast.

Eclogue 12 – December

ARGVMENT.

This Æglogue (euen as the first beganne) is ended with a
complaynte of Colin to God Pan. Wherein as weary of his
former wayes, he proportioneth his life to the foure seasons
of the yeare, comparing hys youthe to the spring time, when
he was fresh and free from loues follye. His manhoode to
the sommer, which he sayth, was consumed with greate
heate and excessiue drouth caused throughe a Comet or
blasinge starre, by which hee meaneth loue, which passion
is comenly compared to such flames and immoderate heate.
His riper yeares hee resembleth to an vnseasonable harueste
wherein the fruites fall ere they be rype. His latter age to
winters chyll and frostie season, now drawing neare to his
last ende.

The gentle shepheard satte beside a springe,
All in the shadowe of a bushye brere,
That *Colin* hight, which wel could pype and singe,
For he of *Tityrus* his songs did lere.
    There as he satte in secreate shade alone,
    Thus gan he make of loue his piteous mone.

O soueraigne *Pan* thou God of shepheards all,
Which of our tender Lambkins takest keepe:
And when our flocks into mischaunce mought fall,
Doest saue from mischiefe the vnwary sheepe:

44

Als of their maisters hast no lesse regarde,
Then of the flocks, which thou doest watch and ward:

I thee beseche (so be thou deigne to heare,
Rude ditties tund to shepheardes Oaten reede,
Or if I euer sonet song so cleare,
As it with pleasaunce mought thy fancie feede)
    Hearken a while from thy greene cabinet,
    The rurall song of carefull Colinet.

Whilome in youth, when flowrd my ioyfull spring,
Like Swallow swift I wandred here and there:
For heate of heedlesse lust me so did sting,
That I of doubted daunger had no feare.
    I went the wastefull woodes and forest wyde.
    Withouten dreade of Wolues to bene espyed.

I wont to raunge amydde the mazie thickette,
And gather nuttes to make me Christmas game:
And ioyed oft to chace the trembling Pricket,
Or hunt the hartlesse hare, til shee were tame.
    What wreaked I of wintrye ages waste,
    Tho deemed I, my spring would euer laste.

How often haue I scaled the craggie Oke,
All to dislodge the Rauen of her neste:
Howe haue I wearied with many a stroke
The stately Walnut tree, the while the rest
    Vnder the tree fell all for nuts at strife:
    For ylike to me was libertee and lyfe.

45

And for I was in thilke same looser yeares,
(Whether the Muse so wrought me from my birth,
Or I to much beleeued my shepherd pères)
Somedele ybent to song and musicks mirth.
    A good olde shephearde, *Wrenock* was his name,
    Made me by arte more cunning in the same.

For thence I durst in derring doe compare
With shepheardes swayne, what euer fedde in field:
And if that *Hobbinol* right iudgement bare,
To *Pan* his owne selfe pype I neede not yield.
    For if the flocking Nymphes did folow *Pan*,
    The wiser Muses after *Colin* ranne.

But ah such pryde at length was ill repayde,
The shepheardes God (perdie God was he none)
My hurtlesse pleasaunce did me ill vpbraide,
My freedome lorne, my life he lefte to mone.
    Loue they him called, that gaue me checkmate,
    But better mought they haue behote him
        Hate.

Tho gan my louely Spring bid me farewel,
And Sommer season sped him to display
(For loue then in the Lyons house did dwell)
The raging fyre, that kindled at his ray.
    A comett stird vp that vnkindly heate,
    That reigned (as men sayd) in *Venus* seate.

Forth was I ledde, not as I wont afore,
When choise I had to choose my wandring waye:
But whether luck and loues vnbridled lore
Would leade me forth on Fancies bitte to playe,
   The bush my bedde, the bramble was my bowre,
   The Woodes can witnesse many a wofull stowre

Where I was wont to seeke the honey Bee,
Working her formall rowmes in Wexen frame:
The grieslie Todestoole growne there mought
    I see
And loathed Paddocks lording on the same.
   And where the chaunting birds luld me a sleepe,
   The ghastlie Owle her grieuous ynne doth keepe.

Then as the springe giues place to elder time,
And bringeth forth the fruite of sommers pryde:
All so my age now passed youngthly pryme,
To thinges of ryper reason selfe applyed.
   And learned of lighter timber cotes to frame,
   Such as might saue my sheepe and me fro shame.

To make fine cages for the Nightingale,
And Baskets of bulrushes was my wont:
Who to entrappe the fish in winding sale
Was better seene, or hurtful beastes to hont?
   I learned als the signes of heauen to ken,
   How *Phœbe* fayles, where *Venus* sittes and when.

And tryed time yet taught me greater thinges,
The sodain rysing of the raging seas:
The soothe of byrds by beating of their wings,
The power of herbs, both which can hurt and ease:
    And which be wont t'enrage the restlesse sheepe,
    And which be wont to worke eternall sleepe.

But ah vnwise and witlesse *Colin cloute*,
That kydst the hidden kinds of many a wede:
Yet kydst not ene to cure thy sore hart roote,
Whose ranckling wound as yet does rifelye bleede.
    Why liuest thou stil, and yet hast thy deathes
        wound?
    Why dyest thou stil, and yet aliue art founde?

Thus is my sommer worne away and wasted,
Thus is my haruest hastened all to rathe:
The eare that budded faire, is burnt and blasted,
And all my hoped gaine is turnd to scathe.
    Of all the seede, that in my youth was sowne,
    Was nought but brakes and brambles to be mowne.

My boughes with bloosmes that crowned were at firste,
And promised of timely fruite such store,
Are left both bare and barrein now at erst
The flattring fruite is fallen to grownd before,
    And rotted, ere they were halfe mellow ripe:
    My haruest wast, my hope away dyd wipe.

The fragrant flowres, that in my garden grewe,
Bene withered, as they had bene gathered long.
Theyr rootes bene dryed vp for lacke of dewe,
Yet dewed with teares they han be euer among.
    Ah who has wrought my *Rosalind* this spight
      To spil the flowres, that should her girlond dight?

And I, that whilome wont to frame my pype,
Vnto the shifting of the shepheards foote:
Sike follies nowe haue gathered as too ripe
And cast hem out, as rotten and vnsoote.
    The loser Lasse I cast to please nomore,
      One if I please, enough is me therefore.

And thus of all my haruest hope I haue
Nought reaped but a weedye crop of care:
Which, when I thought haue thresht in swelling
    sheaue,
Cockel for corne, and chaffe for barley bare.
    Soone as the chaffe should in the fan be fynd,
      All was blowne away of the wauering wynd.

So now my yeare drawes to his latter terme,
My spring is spent, my sommer burnt vp quite:
My harueste hasts to stirre vp winter sterne,
And bids him clayme with rigorous rage hys right.
    So nowe he stormes with many a sturdy stoure,
      So now his blustring blast eche coste doth scoure.

The carefull cold hath nypt my rugged rynde,
And in my face deepe furrowes eld hath pight:
My head besprent with hoary frost I fynd,
And by myne eie the Crow his clawe dooth wright.
  Delight is layd abedde, and pleasure past,
  No sonne now shines, cloudes han all ouercast.

Now leaue ye shepheardes boyes your merry glee,
My Muse is hoarse and weary of thys stounde:
Here will I hang my pype vpon this tree,
Was neuer pype of reede did better sounde.
  Winter is come, that blowes the bitter blaste,
  And after Winter dreerie death does hast.

Gather ye together my little flocke,
My little flock, that was to me so liefe:
Let me, ah lette me in your folds ye lock,
Ere the breme Winter breede you greater griefe.
  Winter is come, that blowes the balefull breath,
  And after Winter commeth timely death.

Adieu delightes, that lulled me asleepe,
Adieu my deare, whose loue I bought so deare:
Adieu my little Lambes and loued sheepe,
Adieu ye Woodes that oft my witnesse were:
  Adieu good *Hobbinol*, that was so true,
  Tell *Rosalind*, her *Colin* bids her adieu.

From COLIN CLOUTS COME HOME AGAINE

For when I thinke of her, as oft I ought,
Then want I words to speake it fitly forth:
And when I speake of her what I haue thought,
I cannot thinke according to her worth.
Yet will I thinke of her, yet will I speake,
So long as life my limbs doth hold together,
And when as death these vitall bands shall breake,
Her name recorded I will leaue for euer.
Her name in euery tree I will endosse,
That as the trees do grow, her name may grow:
And in the ground each where will it engrosse,
And fill with stones, that all men may it know.
The speaking woods and murmuring waters fall,
Her name Ile teach in knowen termes to frame:
And eke my lambs when for their dams they call,
Ile teach to call for *Cynthia* by name.
And long while after I am dead and rotten:
Amongst the shepheards daughters dancing rownd,
My layes made of her shall not be forgotten.
But sung by them with flowry gyrlonds crownd.
And ye, who so ye be, that shall surviue:
When as ye heare her memory renewed,
Be witnesse of her bountie here aliue,
Which she to *Colin* her poore shepheard shewed.
  Much was the whole assembly of those heards,
Moov'd at his speech, so feelingly he spake:
And stood awhile astonisht at his words,

Till *Thestylis* at last their silence brake,
Saying, Why *Colin*, since thou foundst such grace
With *Cynthia* and all her noble crew:
Why didst thou euer leaue that happie place,
In which such wealth might vnto thee accrew?
And back returnedst to this barrein soyle,
Where cold and care and penury do dwell:
Here to keep sheepe, with hunger and with toyle,
Most wretched he, that is and cannot tell.

  Happie indeed (said *Colin*) I him hold,
That may that blessed presence still enioy,
Of fortune and of enuy vncomptrold,
Which still are wont most happie states t'annoy:
But I by that which little while I prooued:
Some part of those enormities did see,
The which in Court continually hooued,
And followd those which happie seemd to bee.
Therefore I silly man, whose former dayes
Had in rude fields bene altogether spent,
Durst not aduenture such vnknowen wayes,
Nor trust the guile of fortunes blandishment,
But rather chose back to my sheep to tourne,
Whose vtmost hardnesse I before had tryde,
Then hauing learnd repentance late, to mourne
Emongst those wretches which I there descryde.

  Shepheard (said *Thestylis*) it seemes of spight
Thou speakest thus gainst their felicitie,
Which thou enuiest, rather then of right
That ought in them blameworthie thou doest spie.

Cause haue I none (quoth he) of cancred will
To quite them ill, that me demeand so well:
But selfe-regard of priuate good or ill,
Moues me of each, so as I found, to tell,
And eke to warne yong shepheards wandring wit,
Which through report of that liues painted blisse,
Abandon quiet home, to seeke for it,
And leaue their lambes to losse, misled amisse.
For sooth to say, it is no sort of life,
For shepheard fit to lead in that same place,
Where each one seeks with malice and with strife,
To thrust downe other into foule disgrace,
Himselfe to raise: and he doth soonest rise
That best can handle his deceitfull wit,
In subtil shifts, and finest sleights deuise,
Either by slaundring his well deemed name,
Through leasings lewd, and fained forgerie:
Or else by breeding him some blot of blame,
By creeping close into his secrecie;
To which him needs a guilefull hollow hart,
Masked with faire dissembling curtesie,
A filed toung furnisht with tearmes of art,
No art of schoole, but Courtiers schoolery.
For arts of schoole haue there small countenance,
Counted but toyes to busie ydle braines,
And there professours find small maintenance,
But to be instruments of others gaines.
Ne is there place for any gentle wit,
Vnlesse to please, it selfe it can applie:

But shouldred is, or out of doore quite shit,
As base, or blunt, vnmeet for melodie.
For each mans worth is measured by his weed,
As harts by hornes, or asses by their eares:
Yet asses been not all whose eares exceed,
Nor yet all harts, that hornes the highest beares.
For highest lookes haue not the highest mynd,
Nor haughtie words most full of highest thoughts:
But are like bladders blowen vp with wynd,
That being prickt do vanish into noughts.
Euen such is all their vaunted vanitie,
Nought else but smoke, that fumeth soone away;
Such is their glorie that in simple eie
Seeme greatest, when their garments are most gay.
So they themselues for praise of fooles do sell,
And all their wealth for painting on a wall;
With price whereof, they buy a golden bell,
And purchace highest rowmes in bowre and hall:
Whiles single Truth and simple honestie
Do wander vp and downe despys'd of all;
Their plaine attire such glorious gallantry
Disdaines so much, that none them in doth call.

From THE FAERIE QUEENE
Book 3, Canto I
PROLOGUE

1

It falls me here to write of Chastity,
   That fairest vertue, farre aboue the rest;
   For which what needs me fetch from *Faery*
   Forreine ensamples, it to haue exprest?
   Sith it is shrined in my Soueraines brest,
   And form'd so liuely in each perfect part,
   That to all Ladies, which haue it profest,
   Need but behold the pourtraict of her hart,
If pourtrayd it might be by any liuing art.

2

But liuing art may not least part expresse,
   Nor life-resembling pencill it can paint,
   All were it *Zeuxis* or *Praxiteles*:
   His dædale hand would faile, and greatly faint,
   And her perfections with his error taint:
   Ne Poets wit, that passeth Painter farre
   In picturing the parts of beautie daint,
   So hard a workmanship aduenture darre,
For fear through want of words her excellence to
   marre.

3

How then shall I, Apprentice of the skill,
  That whylome in diuinest wits did raine,
  Presume so high to stretch mine humble quill?
  Yet now my lucklesse lot doth me constraine
  Hereto perforce. But O dred Soueraine
  Thus farre forth pardon, sith that choicest wit
  Cannot your glorious pourtraict figure plaine
  That I in colourd showes may shadow it,
And antique praises vnto present persons fit.

4

But if in liuing colours, and right hew,
  Your selfe you couet to see pictured,
  Who can it doe more liuely, or more trew,
  Then that sweet verse, with *Nectar* sprinckeled,
  In which a gracious seruant pictured
  His *Cynthia*, his heauens fairest light?
  That with his melting sweetnesse rauished,
  And with the wonder of her beames bright,
My senses lulled are in slomber of delight.

5

But let that same delitious Poet lend
  A little leaue vnto a rusticke Muse
  To sing his mistresse prayse, and let him mend,
  If ought amis her liking may abuse:
  Ne let his fairest *Cynthia* refuse,
  In mirrours more then one her selfe to see,
  But either *Gloriana* let her chuse,
  Or in *Belphœbe* fashioned to bee:
In th'one her rule, in th'other her rare chastitee.

CANTO I

Guyon encountreth Britomart,
faire Florimell is chaced:
Duessaes traines and Malecastaes
champions are defaced.

1

The famous Briton Prince and Faerie knight,
  After long wayes and perilous paines endured,
  Hauing their wearie limbes to perfect plight
  Restord, and sory wounds right well recured,
  Of the faire *Alma* greatly were procured,
  To make there lenger soiourne and abode;
  But when thereto they might not be allured,
  From seeking praise, and deeds of armes abrode,
They courteous conge tooke, and forth together yode.

2

But the captiu'd *Acrasia* he sent,
  Because of trauell long, a nigher way,
  With a strong gard, all reskew to preuent,
  And her to Faerie court safe to conuay,
  That her for witnesse of his hard assay,
  Vnto his *Faerie* Queene he might present:
  But he him selfe betooke another way,
  To make more triall of his hardiment,
And seeke aduentures, as he with Prince *Arthur* went.

3

Long so they trauelled through wastefull wayes,
  Where daungers dwelt, and perils most did wonne,
  To hunt for glorie and renowmed praise;
  Full many Countries they did ouerronne,
  From the vprising to the setting Sunne,
  And many hard aduentures did atchieue;
  Of all the which they honour euer wonne,
  Seeking the weake oppressed to relieue,
And to recouer right for such, as wrong did grieue.

4

At last as through an open plaine they yode,
  They spide a knight, that towards pricked faire,
  And him beside an aged Squire there rode,
  That seem'd to couch vnder his shield three-square,
  As if that age bad him that burden spare,
  And yield it those, that stouter could it wield:
  He them espying, gan himselfe prepare,
  And on his arme addresse his goodly shield
That bore a Lion passant in a golden field.

Which seeing good Sir *Guyon*, deare besought
   The Prince of grace, to let him runne that turne.
   He graunted: then the Faery quickly raught
   His poinant speare, and sharpely gan to spurne
   His fomy steed, whose fierie feete did burne
   The verdant grasse, as he thereon did tread;
   Ne did the other backe his foot returne,
   But fiercely forward came withouten dread,
And bent his dreadfull speare against the others head.

They bene ymet, and both their points arriued,
   But *Guyon* droue so furious and fell,
   That seem'd both shield and plate it would haue
      riued;
   Nathelesse it bore his foe not from his sell,
   But made him stagger, as he were not well:
   But *Guyon* selfe, ere well he was aware,
   Nigh a speares length behind his crouper fell,
   Yet in his fall so well him selfe he bare,
That mischieuous mischance his life and limbes did
   spare.

Great shame and sorrow of that fall he tooke;
   For neuer yet, sith warlike armes he bore,
   And shiuering speare in bloudie field first shooke,
   He found himselfe dishonored so sore.
   Ah gentlest knight, that euer armour bore,
   Let not thee grieue dismounted to haue beene,
   And brought to ground, that neuer wast before;
   For not thy fault, but secret powre vnseene,
That speare enchaunted was, which layd thee on the
   greene.

8

But weenedst thou what wight thee ouerthrew,
   Much greater griefe and shamefuller regret
   For thy hard fortune then thou wouldst renew,
   That of a single damzell thou wert met
   On equall plaine, and there so hard beset;
   Euen the famous *Britomart* it was,
   Whom straunge aduenture did from *Britaine* fet,
   To seeke her louer (loue farre sought alas,)
Whose image she had seene in *Venus* looking glas.

9

Full of disdainefull wrath, he fierce vprose,
   For to reuenge that foule reprochfull shame,
   And snatching his bright sword began to close
   With her on foot, and stoutly forward came;
   Die rather would he, then endure that same.
   Which when his Palmer saw, he gan to feare
   His toward perill and vntoward blame,
   Which by that new rencounter he should reare:
For death sate on the point of that enchaunted speare.

10

And hasting towards him gan faire perswade,
   Not to prouoke misfortune, nor to weene
   His speares default to mend with cruell blade;
   For by his mightie Science he had seene
   The secret vertue of that weapon keene,
   That mortall puissance mote not withstond:
   Nothing on earth mote alwaies happie beene.
   Great hazard were it, and aduenture fond,
To loose long gotten honour with one euill hond.

11

By such good meanes he him discounselled,
  From prosecuting his reuenging rage;
  And eke the Prince like treaty handeled,
  His wrathfull will with reason to asswage,
  And laid the blame, not to his carriage,
  But to his starting steed, that swaru'd asyde,
  And to the ill purueyance of his page,
  That had his furnitures not firmely tyde:
So is his angry courage fairely pacifyde.

12

Thus reconcilement was betweene them knit,
  Through goodly temperance, and affection chaste,
  And either vowd with all their power and wit,
  To let not others honour be defaste,
  Of friend or foe, who euer it embaste,
  Ne armes to beare against the others syde:
  In which accord the Prince was also plaste,
  And with that golden chaine of concord tyde.
So goodly all agreed, they forth yfere did ryde.

13

O goodly vsage of those antique times,
   In which the sword was seruant vnto right;
   When not for malice and contentious crimes,
   But all for praise, and proofe of manly might,
   The martiall brood accustomed to fight:
   Then honour was the meed of victorie,
   And yet the vanquished had no despight:
   Let later age that noble vse enuie,
Vile rancour to auoid, and cruell surquedrie.

14

Long they thus trauelled in friendly wise,
   Through countries waste, and eke well edifyde,
   Seeking aduentures hard, to exercise
   Their puissance, whylome full dernely tryde:
   At length they came into a forrest wyde,
   Whose hideous horror and sad trembling sound
   Full griesly seem'd: Therein they long did ryde,
   Yet tract of liuing creatures none they found,
Saue Beares, Lions, and Buls, which romed them
   around.

15

All suddenly out of the thickest brush,
  Vpon a milk-white Palfrey all alone,
  A goodly Ladie did foreby them rush,
  Whose face did seeme as cleare as Christall stone,
  And eke through feare as white as whales bone:
  Her garments all were wrought of beaten gold,
  And all her steed with tinsell trappings shone,
  Which fled so fast, that nothing mote him hold,
And scarse them leasure gaue, her passing to behold.

16

Still as she fled, her eye she backward threw,
  As fearing euill, that pursewd her fast;
  And her faire yellow locks behind her flew,
  Loosely disperst with puffe of euery blast:
  All as a blazing starre doth farre outcast
  His hearie beames, and flaming lockes dispred
  At sight whereof the people stand aghast:
  But the sage wisard telles, as he has red,
That it importunes death and dolefull drerihed.

17

So as they gazed after her a while,
  Lo where a griesly Foster forth did rush,
  Breathing out beastly lust her to defile:
  His tyreling iade he fiercely forth did push,
  Through thicke and thin, both ouer banke and
    bush
  In hope her to attaine by hooke or crooke,
  That from his gorie sides the bloud did gush:
  Large were his limbes, and terrible his looke,
And in his clownish hand a sharp bore speare he
  shooke.

18

Which outrage when those gentle knights did see,
  Full of great enuie and fell gealosy,
  They stayd not to auise, who first should bee,
  But all spurd after fast, as they mote fly,
  To reskew her from shamefull villany.
  The Prince and *Guyon* equally byliue
  Her selfe pursewd, in hope to win thereby
  Most goodly meede, the fairest Dame aliue:
But after the foule foster *Timias* did striue.

19

The whiles faire *Britomart*, whose constant mind,
  Would not so lightly follow beauties chace,
  Ne reckt of Ladies Loue, did stay behind,
  And them awayted there a certaine space,
  To weet if they would turne backe to that place:
  But when she saw them gone, she forward went,
  As lay her iourney, through that perlous Pace,
  With stedfast courage and stout hardiment;
Ne euill thing she fear'd, ne euill thing she ment.

20

At last as nigh out of the wood she came,
  A stately Castle farre away she spyde,
  To which her steps directly she did frame.
  That Castle was most goodly edifyde,
  And plaste for pleasure nigh that forrest syde:
  But faire before the gate a spatious plaine,
  Mantled with greene, it selfe did spredden wyde,
  On which she saw sixe knights, that did darraine
Fierce battell against one, with cruell might and
  maine.

21

Mainly they all attonce vpon him laid,
  And sore beset on euery side around,
  That nigh he breathlesse grew, yet nought dismaid,
  Ne euer to them yielded foot of ground
  All had he lost much bloud through many a
     wound,
  But stoutly dealt his blowes, and euery way
  To which he turned in his wrathfull stound,
  Made them recoile, and fly from dred decay,
That none of all the sixe before, him durst assay.

22

Like dastard Curres, that hauing at a bay
  The saluage beast embost in wearie chace,
  Dare not aduenture on the stubborne pray,
  Ne byte before, but rome from place to place,
  To get a snatch, when turned is his face.
  In such distresse and doubtfull ieopardy,
  When *Britomart* him saw, she ran a pace
  Vnto his reskew, and with earnest cry,
Bad those same sixe forbeare that single enimy.

23

But to her cry they list not lenden eare,
   Ne ought the more their mightie strokes surceasse,
   But gathering him round about more neare,
   Their direfull rancour rather did encreasse;
   Till that she rushing through the thickest preasse,
   Perforce disparted their compacted gyre,
   And soone compeld to hearken vnto peace:
   Tho gan she myldly of them to inquyre
The cause of their dissention and outrageous yre.

Whereto that single knight did answere frame;
   These sixe would me enforce by oddes of might,
   To chaunge my liefe, and loue another Dame,
   That death me liefer were, then such despight,
   So vnto wrong to yield my wrested right:
   For I loue one, the truest one on ground,
   Nelist me chaunge; she th' *Errant Damzell* hight,
   For whose deare sake full many a bitter stownd,
I haue endur'd, and tasted many a bloudy wound.

Certes (said she) then bene ye sixe to blame,
  To weene your wrong by force to iustifie:
  For knight to leaue his Ladie were great shame,
  That faithfull is, and better were to die.
  All losse is lesse, and lesse the infamie,
  Then losse of loue to him, that loues but one;
  Ne may loue be compeld by maisterie;
  For soone as maisterie comes, sweet loue anone
Taketh his nimble wings, and soone away is gone.

Then spake one of those sixe, There dwelleth here
  Within this castle wall a Ladie faire,
  Whose soueraine beautie hath no liuing pere.
  Thereto so bounteous and so debonaire,
  That neuer any mote with her compaire.
  She hath ordaind this law, which we approue,
  That euery knight, which doth this way repaire,
  In case he haue no Ladie, nor no loue,
Shall doe vnto her seruice neuer to remoue.

But if he haue a Ladie or a Loue,
   Then must he her forgoe with foule defame,
   Or else with vs by dint of sword approue,
   That she is fairer, then our fairest Dame,
   As did this knight, before ye hither came.
   Perdie (said *Britomart*) the choise is hard:
   But what reward had he, that ouercame?
   He should aduaunced be to high regard,
(Said they) and haue our Ladies loue for his reward.

28

Therefore aread Sir, if thou haue a loue.
   Loue haue I sure, (quoth she) but Lady none;
   Yet will I not fro mine owne loue remoue,
   Ne to your Lady will I seruice done,
   But wreake your wrongs wrought to this knight
     alone,
   And proue his cause. With that her mortall speare
   She mightily auentred towards one,
   And downe him smot, ere well aware he weare,
Then to the next she rode, and downe the next did
   beare.

29

Ne did she stay, till three on ground she layd
  That none of them himselfe could reare againe,
  The fourth was by that other knight dismayd,
  All were he wearie of his former paine,
  That now there do but two of six remaine;
  Which two did yield, before she did them smight.
  Ah (said she then) now may ye all see plaine,
  That truth is strong, and trew loue most of might,
That for his trusty seruaunts doth so strongly fight.

30

Too well we see, (said they) and proue too well
  Our faulty weaknesse, and your matchlesse might:
  For thy, faire Sir, yours be the Damozell,
  Which by her owne law to your lot doth light,
  And we your liege men faith vnto you plight.
  So vnderneath her feet their swords they mard,
  And after her besought, well as they might,
  To enter in, and reape the dew reward:
She graunted, and then in they all together far'd.

31

Long were it to describe the goodly frame,
   And stately port of *Castle Ioyeous*,
   (For so that Castle hight by commune name)
   Where they were entertaind with curteous
   And comely glee of many gracious
   Faire Ladies, and of many a gentle knight,
   Who through a Chamber long and spacious,
   Eftsoones them brought vnto their Ladies sight,
That of them cleeped was the *Lady of delight*.

32

But for to tell the sumptuous aray
   Of that great chamber, should be labour lost:
   For liuing wit, I weene, cannot display
   The royall riches and exceeding cost,
   Of euery pillour and of euery post;
   Which all of purest bullion framed were,
   And with great pearles and pretious stones embost,
   That the bright glister of their beames cleare
Did sparckle forth great light, and glorious did
   appeare.

33

These straunger knights through passing, forth were
   led
  Into an inner rowme, whose royaltee
  And rich purueyance might vneath be red;
  Mote Princes place beseeme so deckt to bee.
  Which stately manner when as they did see,
  The image of superfluous riotize,
  Exceeding much the state of meane degree,
  They greatly wondered, whence so sumptuous guize
Might be maintaynd, and each gan diuersely deuize.

The wals were round about apparelled
  With costly clothes of *Arras* and of *Toure*,
  In which with cunning hand was pourtrahed
  The loue of *Venus* and her Paramoure
  The faire *Adonis*, turned to a flowre,
  A worke of rare deuice, and wondrous wit.
  First did it shew the bitter balefull stowre,
  Which her assayd with many a feruent fit,
When first her tender hart was with his beautie smit.

Then with what sleights and sweet allurements she
   Entyst the Boy, as well that art she knew,
   And wooed him her Paramoure to be;
   Now making girlonds of each flowre that grew,
   To crowne his golden lockes with honour dew;
   Now leading him into a secret shade
   From his Beauperes, and from bright heauens vew,
   Where him to sleepe she gently would perswade,
Or bathe him in a fountaine by some couert glade.

36

And whilst he slept, she ouer him would spred
   Her mantle, colour'd like the starry skyes,
   And her soft arme lay vnderneath his hed,
   And with ambrosiall kisses bathe his eyes;
   And whilest he bath'd, with her two crafty spyes,
   She secretly would search each daintie lim,
   And throw into the well sweet Rosemaryes,
   And fragrant violets, and Pances trim,
And euer with sweet Nectar she did sprinkle him.

37

So did she steale his heedelesse hart away,
   And ioyd his loue in secret vnespyde.
   But for she saw him bent to cruell play,
   To hunt the saluage beast in forrest wyde,
   Dreadfull of daunger, that mote him betyde,
   She oft and oft aduiz'd him to refraine
   From chase of greater beasts, whose brutish pryde
   Mote breede him scath vnwares: but all in vaine;
For who can shun the chaunce, that dest'ny doth
   crdaine?

38

Lo, where beyond he lyeth languishing,
   Deadly engored of a great wild Bore,
   And by his side the Goddesse groueling
   Makes for him endlesse mone, and euermore
   With her soft garment wipes away the gore,
   Which staines his snowy skin with hatefull hew:
   But when she saw no helpe might him restore,
   Him to a dainty flowre she did transmew,
Which in that cloth was wrought, as if it liuely grew.

39

So was that chamber clad in goodly wize,
  And round about it many beds were dight,
  As whilome was the antique worldes guize,
  Some for vntimely ease, some for delight,
  As pleased them to vse, that vse it might:
  And all was full of Damzels, and of Squires,
  Dauncing and reueling both day and night,
  And swimming deepe in sensuall desires,
And *Cupid* still emongst them kindled lustfull fires.

40

And all the while sweet Musicke did diuide
  Her looser notes with *Lydian* harmony;
  And all the while sweet birdes thereto applide
  Their daintie layes and dulcet melody,
  Ay caroling of loue and iollity,
  That wonder was to heare their trim consort.
  Which when those knights beheld, with scornefull
    eye,
  They sdeigned such lasciuious disport,
And loath'd the loose demeanure of that wanton sort.

41

Thence they were brought to that great Ladies vew,
  Whom they found sitting on a sumptuous bed,
  That glistred all with gold and glorious shew,
  As the proud *Persian* Queenes accustomed:
  She seemd a woman of great bountihed,
  And of rare beautie, sauing that askaunce
  Her wanton eyes, ill signes of womanhed,
  Did roll too lightly, and too often glaunce,
Without regard of grace, or comely amenaunce.

42

Long worke it were, and needlesse to deuize
  Their goodly entertainement and great glee:
  She caused them be led in curteous wize
  Into a bowre, disarmed for to bee,
  And cheared well with wine and spiceree:
  The *Redcrosse* Knight was soone disarmed there,
  But the braue Mayd would not disarmed bee,
  But onely vented vp her vmbriere,
And so did let her goodly visage to appere.

43

As when faire *Cynthia*, in darkesome night,
   Is in a noyous cloud enueloped,
   Where she may find the substaunce thin and light,
   Breakes forth her siluer beames, and her bright hed
   Discouers to the world discomfited;
   Of the poore traueller, that went astray,
   With thousand blessings she is heried;
   Such was the beautie and the shining ray,
With which faire *Britomart* gaue light vnto the day.

And eke those six, which lately with her fought,
   Now were disarmd, and did them selues present
   Vnto her vew, and company vnsoght;
   For they all seemed curteous and gent,
   And all sixe brethren, borne of one parent,
   Which had them traynd in all ciuilitee,
   And goodly taught to tilt and turnament;
   Now were they liegemen to this Lady free,
And her knights seruice ought, to hold of her in fee.

The first of them by name *Gardante* hight,
  A iolly person, and of comely vew;
  The second was *Parlante*, a bold knight,
  And next to him *Iocante* did ensew;
  Basciante did him selfe most curteous shew;
  But fierce *Bacchante* seemd too fell and keene;
  And yet in armes *Noctante* greater grew:
    All were faire knights, and goodly well beseene,
But to faire *Britomart* they all but shadowes beene.

For she was full of amiable grace,
  And manly terrour mixed therewithall,
  That as the one stird vp affections bace,
  So th'other did mens rash desires apall,
  And hold them backe, that would in errour fall;
  As he, that hath espide a vermeill Rose,
  To which sharpe thornes and breres the way
    forstall,
    Dare not for dread his hardy hand expose,
But wishing it far off, his idle wish doth lose.

Whom when the Lady saw so faire a wight,
   All ignoraunt of her contrary sex,
   (For she her weend a fresh and lusty knight)
   She greatly gan enamoured to wex,
   And with vaine thoughts her falsed fancy vex:
   Her fickle hart conceiued hasty fire,
   Like sparkes of fire, which fall in sclender flex,
   That shortly brent into extreme desire,
And ransackt all her veines with passion entire.

48

Eftsoones she grew to great impatience
   And into termes of open outrage brust,
   That plaine discouered her incontinence,
   Ne reckt she, who her meaning did mistrust;
   For she was giuen all to fleshly lust,
   And poured forth in sensuall delight,
   That all regard of shame she had discust,
   And meet respect of honour put to flight:
So shamelesse beauty soone becomes a loathly sight.

49

Faire Ladies, that to loue captiued arre,
  And chaste desires do nourish in your mind,
  Let not her fault your sweet affections marre,
  Ne blot the bounty of all womankind;
  'Mongst thousands good one wanton Dame to find:
  Emongst the Roses grow some wicked weeds;
  For this was not to loue, but lust inclind;
  For loue does always bring forth bounteous deeds,
And in each gentle hart desire of honour breeds.

50

Nought so of loue this looser Dame did skill,
  But as a coale to kindle fleshly flame,
  Giuing the bridle to her wanton will,
  And treading vnder foote her honest name:
  Such loue is hate, and such desire is shame.
  Still did she roue at her with crafty glaunce
  Of her false eyes, that at her hart did ayme,
  And told her meaning in her countenaunce;
But *Britomart* dissembled it with ignoraunce.

51

Supper was shortly dight and downe they sat,
  Where they were serued with all sumptuous fare,
  Whiles fruitfull *Ceres*, and *Lyæus* fat
  Pourd out their plenty, without spight or spare:
  Nought wanted there, that dainty was and rare;
  And aye the cups their bancks did ouerflow,
  And aye betweene the cups, she did prepare
  Way to her loue, and secret darts did throw;
But *Britomart* would not such guilfull message know.

52

So when they slaked had the feruent heat
  Of appetite with meates of euery sort,
  The Lady did faire *Britomart* entreat,
  Her to disarme, and with delightfull sport
  To loose her warlike limbs and strong effort,
  But when she mote not thereunto be wonne,
  (For she her sexe vnder that straunge purport
  Did vse to hide, and plaine apparaunce shonne:)
In plainer wise to tell her grieuaunce she begonne.

And all attonce discouered her desire
  With sighes, and sobs, and plaints, and piteous
    griefe,
  The outward sparkes of her in burning fire;
  Which spent in vaine, at last she told her briefe,
  That but if she did lend her short reliefe,
  And do her comfort, she mote algates dye.
  But the chaste damzell, that had neuer priefe
  Of such malengine and fine forgerie,
Did easily beleeue her strong extremitie.

Full easie was for her to haue beliefe,
  Who by self-feeling of her feeble sexe,
  And by long triall of the inward griefe,
  Wherewith imperious loue her hart did vexe,
  Could iudge what paines do louing harts perplexe.
  Who meanes no guile, be guiled soonest shall,
  And to faire semblaunce doth light faith annexe;
  The bird, that knowes not the false fowlers call,
Into his hidden net full easily doth fall.

For thy she would not in discourteise wise.
  Scorne the faire offer of good will profest;
  For great rebuke it is, loue to despise,
  Or rudely sdeigne a gentle harts request;
  But with faire countenaunce, as beseemed best,
  Her entertaynd; nath'lesse she inly deemd
  Her loue too light, to wooe a wandring guest:
  Which she misconstruing, thereby esteemd
That from like inward fire that outward smoke had
  steemd.

Therewith a while she her flit fancy fed,
  Till she mote winne fit time for her desire,
  But yet her wound still inward freshly bled,
  And through her bones the false instilled fire
  Did spred it selfe, and venime close inspire.
  Tho were the tables taken all away,
  And euery knight, and euery gentle Squire
  Gan choose his dame with *Basciomani* gay,
With whom he meant to make his sport and courtly
  play.

Some fell to daunce, some fell to hazardry,
  Some to make loue, some to make meriment,
  As diuerse wits to diuers things apply;
  And all the while faire *Malecasta* bent
  Her crafty engins to her close intent.
  By this th'eternall lampes, wherewith high *Ioue*
  Doth light the lower world, were halfe yspent,
  And the moist daughters of huge *Atlas* stroue
Into the *Ocean* deepe to driue their weary droue.

High time it seemed then for euery wight
  Them to betake vnto their kindly rest;
  Eftsoones long waxen torches weren light,
  Vnto their bowres to guiden euery guest:
  Tho when the Britonesse saw all the rest
  Auoided quite, she gan her selfe despoile,
  And safe commit to her soft fethered nest,
  Where through long watch, and late dayes weary
    toile,
She soundly slept, and carefull thoughts did quite
  assoile.

59

Now whenas all the world in silence deepe
    Yshrowded was, and euery mortall wight
    Was drowned in the depth of deadly sleepe,
    Faire *Malecasta*, whose engrieued spright
    Could find no rest in such perplexed plight,
    Lightly arose out of her wearie bed,
    And vnder the blacke vele of guilty Night,
    Her with a scarlot mantle couered,
That was with gold and Ermines faire enueloped.

60

Then panting soft, and trembling euerie ioynt,
    Her fearfull feete towards the bowre she moued;
    Where she for secret purpose did appoynt
    To lodge the warlike mayd vnwisely loued,
    And to her bed approaching, first she prooued,
    Whether she slept or wakt, with her soft hand
    She softly felt, if any member mooued,
    And lent her wary eare to vnderstand,
If any puffe of breath, or signe of sence she fond.

Which whenas none she fond, with easie shift,
 For feare least her vnwares she should abrayd,
 Th'embroderd quilt she lightly vp did lift,
 And by her side her selfe she softly layd,
 Of euery finest fingers touch affrayd;
 Ne any noise she made, ne word she spake,
 But inly sigh'd. At last the royall Mayd
 Out of her quiet slomber did awake,
And chaungd her weary side, the better ease to take.

Where feeling one close couched by her side,
 She lightly lept out of her filed bed,
 And to her weapon ran, in minde to gride
 The loathed leachour. But the Dame halfe ded
 Through suddein feare and ghastly drerihed,
 Did shrieke alowd, that through the house it rong,
 And the whole family therewith adred,
 Rashly out of their rouzed couches sprong,
And to the troubled chamber all in armes did throng.

63

And those six Knights that Ladies Champions,
  And eke the *Redcrosse* knight ran to the stownd,
  Halfe armd and halfe vnarmd, with them attons:
  Where when confusedly they came, they fownd
  Their Lady lying on the sencelesse grownd;
  On th'other side, they saw the warlike Mayd
  All in her snow-white smocke, with locks vnbownd,
  Threatning the point of her auenging blade,
That with so troublous terrour they were all dismayde.

64

About their Lady first they flockt arownd,
  Whom hauing laid in comfortable couch,
  Shortly they reard out of her frosen swownd;
  And afterwards they gan with fowle reproch
  To stirre vp strife, and troublous contecke broch:
  But by ensample of the last dayes losse,
  None of them rashly durst to her approach,
  Ne in so glorious spoile themselues embosse;
Her succourd eke the Champion of the bloudy Crosse.

But one of those sixe knights, *Gardante* hight,
  Drew out a deadly bow and arrow keene,
  Which forth he sent with felonous despight,
  And fell intent against the virgin sheene:
  The mortall steele stayd not, till it was seene
  To gore her side, yet was the wound not deepe,
  But lightly rased her soft silken skin,
  That drops of purple bloud thereout did weepe,
Which did her lilly smock with staines of vermeil
  steepe.

Wherewith enrag'd she fiercely at them flew,
  And with her flaming sword about her layd,
  That none of them foule mischiefe could eschew,
  But with her dreadfull strokes were all dismayd:
  Here, there, and euery where about her swayd
  Her wrathfull steele, that none mote it abide;
  And eke the *Redcrosse* knight gaue her good aid,
  Ay ioyning foot to foot, and side to side,
That in short space their foes they haue quite terrifide.

Tho whenas all were put to shamefull flight,
   The noble *Britomartis* her arayd,
   And her bright armes about her body dight:
   For nothing would she lenger there be stayd,
   Where so loose life, and so vngentle trade
   Was vsd of Knights and Ladies seeming gent:
   So earely ere the grosse Earthes gryesy shade
   Was all disperst out of the firmament,
They tooke their steeds, and forth vpon their iourney
   went.

From AMORETTI

Fayre eyes, the myrrour of my mazed hart,
   what wondrous vertue is contaynd in you,
   the which both lyfe and death forth from you dart
   into the obiect of your mighty view?
For when ye mildly looke with louely hew,
   then is my soule with life and loue inspired
   but when ye lowre, or looke on me askew,
   then doe I die, as one with lightning fyred.
But since that lyfe is more then death desyred,
   looke euer louely, as becomes you best,
   that your bright beams of my weak eies admyred,
   may kindle liuing fire within my brest.
Such life should be the honor of your light,
   such death the sad ensample of your might.

SONNET. VIII.

More then most faire, full of the liuing fire,
    Kindled aboue vnto the maker neere:
    no eies but ioyes, in which al powers conspire,
    that to the world naught else be counted deare.
Thrugh your bright beames doth not the blinded guest,
    shoot out his darts to base affections wound:
    but Angels come to lead fraile mindes to rest
    in chast desires on heauenly beauty bound.
You frame my thoughts and fashion me within,
    you stop my toung, and teach my hart to speake,
    you calme the storme that passion did begin,
    strong thrugh your cause, but by your vertue weak.
Dark is the world, where your light shined neuer;
    well is he borne, that may behold you euer.

SONNET. IX.

Long-while I sought to what I might compare
    those powrefull eies, which lighten my dark spright,
    yet find I nought on earth to which I dare
    resemble th'ymage of their goodly light.
Not to the Sun: for they doo shine by night;
    nor to the Moone: for they are changed neuer;
    nor to the Starres: for they haue purer sight;
    nor to the fire: for they consume not euer;
Nor to the lightning: for they still perseuer;
    nor to the Diamond: for they are more tender;
    nor vnto Christall: for nought may them seuer;
    nor vnto glasse: such basenesse mought offend her;
Then to the Maker selfe they likest be,
    whose light doth lighten all that here we see.

SONNET. XVI.

One day as I vnwarily did gaze
   on those fayre eyes my loues immortall light:
   the whiles my stonisht hart stood in amaze,
   through sweet illusion of her lookes delight.
I mote perceiue how in her glauncing sight,
   legions of loues with little wings did fly:
   darting their deadly arrowes fyry bright,
   at euery rash beholder passing by.
One of those archers closely I did spy,
   ayming his arrow at my very hart:
   when suddenly with twincle of her eye,
   the Damzell broke his misintended dart.
Had she not so doon, sure I had bene slayne,
   yet as it was, I hardly scap't with paine.

SONNET. XXX.

My loue is lyke to yse, and I to fyre;
   how comes it then that this her cold so great
   is not dissolu'd through my so hot desyre,
   but harder growes the more I her intreat?
Or how comes it that my exceeding heat
   is not delayd by her hart frosen cold:
   but that I burne much more in boyling sweat,
   and feele my flames augmented manifold?
What more miraculous thing may be told
   that fire which all thing melts, should harden yse:
   and yse which is congeald with sencelesse cold,
   should kindle fyre by wonderfull deuyse?
Such is the powre of loue in gentle mind,
   that it can alter all the course of kynd.

SONNET. XXXIV.

Lyke as a ship that through the Ocean wyde,
  by conduct of some star doth make her way,
  whenas a storme hath dimd her trusty guyde,
  out of her course doth wander far astray.
So I whose star, that wont with her bright ray,
  me to direct, with cloudes is ouercast,
  doe wander now in darknesse and dismay,
  through hidden perils round about me plast.
Yet hope I well, that when this storme is past
  my *Helice* the lodestar of my lyfe
  will shine again, and looke on me at last,
  with louely light to cleare my cloudy grief.
Till then I wander carefull comfortlesse,
  in secret sorow and sad pensiuenesse.

What guyle is this, that those her golden tresses,
  She doth attyre vnder a net of gold:
  and with sly skill so cunningly them dresses,
  that which is gold or heare, may scarse be told?
Is it that mens frayle eyes, which gaze too bold,
  she may entangle in that golden snare:
  and being caught may craftily enfold,
  theyr weaker harts, which are not wel aware?
Take heed therefore, myne eyes, how ye doe stare
  henceforth too rashly on that guilefull net,
  in which if euer ye entrapped are,
  out of her bands ye by no meanes shall get.
Fondnesse it were for any being free,
  to couet fetters, though they golden bee.

Is it her nature or is it her will,
    to be so cruell to an humbled foe?
    if nature, then she may it mend with skill,
    if will, then she at will may will forgoe.
But if her nature and her will be so,
    that she will plague the man that loues her most:
    and take delight t'encrease a wretches woe,
    then all her natures goodly guifts are lost.
And that same glorious beauties ydle boast,
    is but a bayt such wretches to beguile:
    as being long in her loues tempest tost,
    she meanes at last to make her piteous spoyle.
O fayrest fayre let neuer it be named,
    that so fayre beauty was so fowly shamed.

SONNET. XLIII.

Shall I then silent be or shall I speake?
  And if I speake, her wrath renew I shall:
  and if I silent be, my hart will breake,
  or choked be with ouerflowing gall.
What tyranny is this both my hart to thrall,
  and eke my toung with proud restraint to tie?
  that nether I may speake nor thinke at all,
  but like a stupid stock in silence die.
Yet I my hart with silence secretly
  will teach to speak, and my iust cause to plead:
  and eke mine eies with meeke humility,
  loue learned letters to her eyes to read.
Which her deep wit, that true harts thought can spel,
  will soone conceiue, and learne to construe well.

SONNET. XLIX.

Fayre cruell, why are ye so fierce and cruell?
  Is it because your eyes haue powre to kill?
    then know, that mercy is the mighties iewell,
    and greater glory thinke to saue, then spill.
But if it be your pleasure and proud will,
    to shew the powre of your imperious eyes:
    then not on him that neuer thought you ill
    but bend your force against your enemyes.
Let them feele th'utmost of your crueltyes,
    and kill with looks, as Cockatrices doo:
    but him that at your footstoole humbled lies,
    with mercifull regard, giue mercy too.
Such mercy shal you make admyred to be,
    so shall you liue by giuing life to me.

Of this worlds Theatre in which we stay,
  My loue lyke the Spectator ydly sits
  beholding me that all the pageants play,
  disguysing diuersly my troubled wits.
Sometimes I ioy when glad occasion fits,
  and mask in myrth lyke to a Comedy:
  soone after when my ioy to sorrow flits,
  I waile and make my woes a Tragedy.
Yet she beholding me with constant eye,
  delights not in my merth nor rues my smart:
  but when I laugh she mocks, and when I cry
  she laughes, and hardens euermore her hart.
What then can moue her? if nor merth nor mone,
  she is no woman, but a sencelesse stone.

The doubt which ye misdeeme, fayre loue, is vaine,
　That fondly feare to loose your liberty,
　when loosing one, two liberties ye gayne,
　and make him bond that bondage earst dyd fly.
Sweet be the bands, the which true loue doth tye,
　without constraynt or dread of any ill:
　the gentle birde feeles no captiuity
　within her cage, but singes and feeds her fill.
There pride dare not approch, nor discord spill
　the league twixt them, that loyal loue hath bound:
　but simple truth and mutuall good will,
　seekes with sweet peace to salue each others wound:
There fayth doth fearlesse dwell in brasen towre,
　and spotlesse pleasure builds her sacred bowre.

Lyke as a huntsman after weary chace,
   Seeing the game from him escapt away,
   sits downe to rest him in some shady place,
   with panting hounds beguiled of their pray:
So after long pursuit and vaine assay,
   when I all weary had the chace forsooke,
   the gentle deare returned the selfe-same way,
   thinking to quench her thirst at the next brooke.
There she beholding me with mylder looke,
   sought not to fly, but fearelesse still did bide:
   till I in hand her yet halfe trembling tooke,
   and with her owne goodwill hir fyrmely tyde.
Strange thing me seemed to see a beast so wyld,
   so goodly wonne with her owne will beguyld.

Oft when my spirit doth spred her bolder winges,
   In mind to mount vp to the purest sky:
     it down is weighd with thoght of earthly things
    and clogd with burden of mortality,
Where when that soueraine beauty it doth spy,
   resembling heauens glory in her light:
     drawne with sweet pleasures bayt, it back doth fly,
    and vnto heauen forgets her former flight.
There my fraile fancy fed with full delight,
   doth bath in blisse and mantleth most at ease:
     ne thinks of other heauen, but how it might
    her harts desire with most contentment please.
Hart need not with none other happinesse,
   but here on earth to haue such heuens blisse.

SONNET. LXXV.

One day I wrote her name vpon the strand,
   but came the waues and washed it away:
   agayne I wrote it with a second hand,
   but came the tyde, and made my paynes his pray.
Vayne man, sayd she, that doest in vaine assay,
   a mortall thing so to immortalize,
   for I my selue shall lyke to this decay,
   and eek my name bee wyped out lykewize.
Not so, (quod I) let baser things deuize
   to dy in dust, but you shall liue by fame:
   my verse your vertues rare shall eternize,
   and in the heuens wryte your glorious name.
Where whenas death shall all the world subdew,
   our loue shall liue, and later life renew.

Men call you fayre, and you doe credit it,
  For that your selfe ye dayly such doe see:
    but the trew fayre, that is the gentle wit,
    and vertuous mind, is much more praysd of me.
For all the rest, how euer fayre it be.
    shall turne to nought and loose that glorious hew:
    but onely that is permanent and free
    from frayle corruption, that doth flesh ensew
That is true beautie: that doth argue you
    to be diuine and borne of heauenly seed:
    deriu'd from that fayre Spirit, from whom al true
    and perfect beauty did at first proceed.
He onely fayre, and what he fayre hath made,
  all other fayre lyke flowers vntymely fade.

SONNET. LXXXIV.

Let not one sparke of filthy lustfull fyre
    breake out, that may her sacred peace molest:
    ne one light glance of sensuall desyre
    Attempt to work her gentle mindes vnrest.
But pure affections bred in spotlesse brest,
    and modest thoughts breathd from wel tempred sprites
    goe visit her in her chast bowre of rest,
    accompanyde with angelick delightes.
There fill your selfe with those most ioyous sights,
    the which my selfe could neuer yet attayne:
    but speake no word to her of these sad plights,
    which her too constant stiffenesse doth constrayn.
Onely behold her rare perfection,
    and blesse your fortunes fayre election.

Since I haue lackt the comfort of that light,
   The which was wont to lead my thoughts astray:
    I wander as in darkenesse of the night,
      affrayd of euery dangers least dismay.
Ne ought I see, though in the clearest day,
   when others gaze vpon theyr shadowes vayne:
   but th'onely image of that heauenly ray,
    whereof some glance doth in mine eie remayne.
Of which beholding the Idæa playne,
   through contemplation of my purest part:
   with light thereof I doe my selfe sustayne,
   and thereon feed my loue-affamisht hart.
But with such brightnesse whylest I fill my mind,
   I starue my body and mine eyes doe blynd.

EPITHALAMION

Ye learned sisters which haue oftentimes
Beene to me ayding, others to adorne:
Whom ye thought worthy of your gracefull rymes,
That euen the greatest did not greatly scorne
To heare theyr names sung in your simple layes,
But ioyed in theyr prayse.
And when ye list your owne mishaps to mourne,
Which death, or loue, or fortunes wreck did rayse,
Your string could soone to sadder tenor turne,
And teach the woods and waters to lament
Your dolefull dreriment.
Now lay those sorrowfull complaints aside,
And hauing all your heads with girland crownd,
Helpe me mine owne loues prayses to resound,
Ne let the same of any be enuide:
So Orpheus did for his owne bride,
So I vnto my selfe alone will sing,
The woods shall to me answer and my Eccho ring.

Early before the worlds light giuing lampe,
His golden beame vpon the hils doth spred,
Hauing disperst the nights vnchearefull dampe,
Doe ye awake, and with fresh lusty hed,
Go to the bowre of my beloued loue,
My truest turtle doue,
Bid her awake; for Hymen is awake,
And long since ready forth his maske to moue,

With his bright Tead that flames with many a flake,
And many a bachelor to waite on him,
In theyr fresh garments trim.
Bid her awake therefore and soone her dight,
For lo the wished day is come at last,
That shall for al the paynes and sorrowes past,
Pay to her vsury of long delight:
And whylest she doth her dight,
Doe ye to her of ioy and solace sing,
That all the woods may answer and your eccho ring.

Bring with you all the Nymphes that you can heare
Both of the riuers and the forrests greene:
And of the sea that neighbours to her neare,
Al with gay girlands goodly wel beseene.
And let them also with them bring in hand,
Another gay girland
For my fayre loue of lillyes and of roses,
Bound trueloue wize with a blew silke riband.
And let them make great store of bridale poses,
And let them eeke bring store of other flowers
To deck the bridale bowers.
And let the ground whereas her foot shall tread,
For feare the stones her tender foot should wrong
Be strewed with fragrant flowers all along,
And diapred lyke the discolored mead.
Which done, doe at her chamber dore awayt,
For she will waken strayt,
The whiles doe ye this song vnto her sing,

The woods shall to you answer and your Eccho ring.

Ye Nymphes of Mulla which with carefull heed,
The siluer scaly trouts doe tend full well,
And greedy pikes which vse therein to feed,
(Those trouts and pikes all others doo excell)
And ye likewise which keepe the rushy lake,
Where none doo fishes take,
Bynd vp the locks the which hang scatterd light,
And in his waters which your mirror make,
Behold your faces as the christall bright,
That when you come whereas my loue doth lie,
No blemish she may spie.
And eke ye lightfoot mayds which keepe the deere,
That on the hoary mountayne vse to towre,
And the wylde wolues which seeke them to deuoure,
With your steele darts doo chace from comming neer
Be also present heere,
To helpe to decke her and to help to sing,
That all the woods may answer and your eccho ring.

Wake, now my loue, awake; for it is time,
The rosy Morne long since left Tithones bed,
All ready to her siluer coche to clyme,
And Phœbus gins to shew his glorious hed.
Hark how the cheerefull birds do chaunt theyr laies
And carroll of loues praise.
The merry Larke hir mattins sings aloft,
The thrush replyes, the Mauis descant playes.

The Ouzell shrills, the Ruddock warbles soft,
So goodly all agree with sweet consent,
To this dayes merriment.
Ah my deere loue why doe ye sleepe thus long,
When meeter were that ye should now awake,
T'awayt the comming of your ioyous make,
And hearken to the birds louelearned song,
The deawy leaues among.
For they of ioy and pleasance to you sing,
That all the woods them answer and theyr eccho ring.

My loue is now awake out of her dreame,
And her fayre eyes like stars that dimmed were
With darksome cloud, now shew theyr goodly beams
More bright then Hesperus his head doth rere.
Come now ye damzels, daughters of delight,
Helpe quickly her to dight,
But first come ye fayre houres which were begot
In Ioues sweet paradice, of Day and Night,
Which doe the seasons of the yeare allot,
And al that euer in this world is fayre
Doe make and still repayre.
And ye three handmayds of the Cyprian Queene,
The which doe still adorne her beauties pride,
Helpe to addorne my beautifullest bride:
And as ye her array, still throw betweene
Some graces to be seene,
And as ye vse to Venus, to her sing,
The whiles the woods shal answer and your eccho ring.

113

Now is my loue all ready forth to come,
Let all the virgins therefore well awayt,
And ye fresh boyes that tend vpon her groome
Prepare your selues; for he is comming strayt.
Set all your things in seemely good aray
Fit for so ioyfull day,
The ioyfulst day that euer sunne did see.
Faire Sun, shew forth thy fauourable ray,
And let thy lifull heat not feruent be
For feare of burning her sunshyne face,
Her beauty to disgrace.
O fayrest Phœbus, father of the Muse,
If euer I did honour thee aright,
Or sing the thing, that mote thy mind delight,
Doe not thy seruants simple boone refuse,
But let this day let this one day be myne,
Let all the rest be thine.
Then I thy souerayne prayses loud wil sing,
That all the woods shal answer and theyr eccho ring.

Harke how the Minstrels gin to shrill aloud
Their merry Musick that resounds from far,
The pipe, the tabor, and the trembling Croud,
That well agree withouten breach or iar.
But most of all the Damzels doe delite,
When they their tymbrels smyte,
And thereunto doe daunce and carrol sweet,
That all the sences they doe rauish quite,
The whyles the boyes run vp and downe the street,

Crying aloud with strong confused noyce,
As if it were one voyce.
Hymen io Hymen, Hymen they do shout,
That euen to the heauens theyr shouting shrill
Doth reach, and all the firmament doth fill,
To which the people standing all about,
As in approuance doe thereto applaud
And loud aduaunce her laud,
And euermore they Hymen Hymen sing,
That all the woods them answer and theyr eccho ring.

Loe where she comes along with portly pace
Lyke Phœbe from her chamber of the East,
Arysing forth to run her mighty race,
Clad all in white, that seemes a virgin best.
So well it her beseemes that ye would weene
Some angell she had beene.
Her long loose yellow locks lyke golden wyre,
Sprinckled with perle, and perling flowres a tweene,
Doe lyke a golden mantle her attyre,
And being crowned with a girland greene,
Seeme lyke some mayden Queene.
Her modest eyes abashed to behold
So many gazers, as on her do stare,
Vpon the lowly ground affixed are.
Ne dare lift vp her countenance too bold,
But blush to heare her prayses sung so loud,
So farre from being proud.
Nathlesse doe ye still loud her prayses sing.

That all the woods may answer and your eccho ring.

Tell me ye merchants daughters did ye see
So fayre a creature in your towne before,
So sweet, so louely, and so mild as she,
Adornd with beautyes grace and vertues store,
Her goodly eyes lyke Saphyres shining bright,
Her forehead yuory white,
Her cheekes lyke apples which the sun hath rudded,
Her lips lyke cherryes charming men to byte,
Her brest like to a bowle of creame vncrudded,
Her paps lyke lyllies budded,
Her snowie necke lyke to a marble towre,
And all her body like a pallace fayre,
Ascending vppe with many a stately stayre,
To honors seat and chastities sweet bowre.
Why stand ye still ye virgins in amaze,
Vpon her so to gaze,
Whiles ye forget your former lay to sing,
To which the woods did answer and your eccho ring.

Bvt if ye saw that which no eyes can see,
The inward beauty of her liuely spright,
Garnisht with heauenly guifts of high degree,
Much more then would ye wonder at that sight,
And stand astonisht lyke to those which red
Medusaes mazeful hed.
There dwels sweet loue and constant chastity,
Vnspotted fayth and comely womanhood,

Regard of honour and mild modesty,
There vertue raynes as Queene in royal throne,
And giueth lawes alone.
The which the base affections doe obay,
And yeeld theyr seruices vnto her will,
Ne thought of thing vncomely euer may
Thereto approch to tempt her mind to ill.
Had ye once seene these her celestial threasures,
And vnreuealed pleasures,
Then would ye wonder and her prayses sing,
That al the woods should answer and your echo ring.

Open the temple gates vnto my loue,
Open them wide that she may enter in,
And all the postes adorne as doth behoue,
And all the pillours deck with girlands trim,
For to recyue this Saynt with honour dew,
That commeth in to you.
With trembling steps and humble reuerence,
She commeth in, before th'almighties vew,
Of her ye virgins learne obedience,
When so ye come into those holy places,
To humble your proud faces:
Bring her vp to th'high altar, that she may
The sacred ceremonies there partake,
The which do endlesse matrimony make,
And let the roring Organs loudly play
The praises of the Lord in liuely notes,
The whiles with hollow throates

The Choristers the ioyous Antheme sing,
That al the woods may answere and their eccho ring.

Behold whiles she before the altar stands
Hearing the holy priest that to her speakes
And blesseth her with his two happy hands,
How the red roses flush vp in her cheekes,
And the pure snow with goodly vermill stayne,
Like crimsin dyde in grayne,
That euen th'Angels which continually,
About the sacred Altare doe remaine,
Forget their seruice and about her fly,
Ofte peeping in her face that seemes more fayre,
The more they on it stare.
But her sad eyes still fastened on the ground,
Are gouerned with goodly modesty,
That suffers not one looke to glaunce awry,
Which may let in a little thought vnsownd.
Why blush ye loue to giue to me your hand,
The pledge of all our band?
Sing ye sweet Angels, Alleluya sing,
That all the woods may answere and your eccho ring.

Now al is done; bring home the bride againe,
Bring home the triumph of our victory,
Bring home with you the glory of her gaine,
With ioyance bring her and with iollity.
Neuer had man more ioyfull day then this,
Whom heauen would heape with blis.

Make feast therefore now all this liue long day,
This day for euer to me holy is,
Poure out the wine without restraint or stay,
Poure not by cups, but by the belly full,
Poure out to all that wull,
And sprinkle all the postes and wals with wine,
That they may sweat, and drunken be withall.
Crowne ye God Bacchus with a coronall,
And Hymen also crowne with wreathes of vine,
And let the Graces daunce vnto the rest;
For they can doo it best:
The whiles the maydens doe theyr carroll sing,
To which the woods shal answer and theyr eccho ring.

Ring ye the bels, ye yong men of the towne,
And leaue your wonted labors for this day:
This day is holy; doe ye write it downe,
That ye for euer it remember may.
This day the sunne is in his chiefest hight,
With Barnaby the bright,
From whence declining daily by degrees,
He somewhat loseth of his heat and light,
When once the Crab behind his back he sees.
But for this time it ill ordained was,
To chose the longest day in all the yeare,
And shortest night, when longest fitter weare:
Yet neuer day so long, but late would passe.
Ring ye the bels, to make it weare away,
And bonefiers make all day,

And daunce about them, and about them sing:
that all the woods may answer, and your eccho ring.

Ah when will this long weary day haue end,
And lende me leaue to come vnto my loue?
How slowly do the houres theyr numbers spend?
How slowly does sad Time his feathers moue?
Hast thee O fayrest Planet to thy home
Within the Westerne fome:
Thy tyred steedes long since haue need of rest.
Long though it be, at last I see it gloome,
And the bright euening star with golden creast
Appeare out of the East.
Fayre childe of beauty, glorious lampe of loue
That all the host of heauen in rankes doost lead,
And guydest louers through the nightes dread,
How chearefully thou lookest from aboue,
And seemst to laugh atweene thy twinkling light
As ioying in the sight
Of these glad many which for ioy doe sing,
That all the woods them answer and their echo ring.

Now ceasse ye damsels your delights forepast;
Enough is it, that all the day was youres:
Now day is doen, and night is nighing fast:
Now bring the Bryde into the brydall boures.
Now night is come, now soone her disaray,
And in her bed her lay;
Lay her in lillies and in violets,

120

And silken courteins ouer her display,
And odourd sheetes, and Arras couerlets.
Behold how goodly my faire loue does ly
In proud humility;
Like vnto Maia, when as Ioue her tooke,
In Tempe, lying on the flowry gras,
Twixt sleepe and wake, after she weary was,
With bathing in the Acidalian brooke.
Now it is night, ye damsels may be gon,
And leaue my loue alone,
And leaue likewise your former lay to sing:
The woods no more shal answere, nor your echo ring.

Now welcome night, thou night so long expected,
That long daies labour doest at last defray,
And all my cares, which cruell loue collected,
Hast sumd in one, and cancelled for aye:
Spread thy broad wing ouer my loue and me,
That no man may vs see,
And in thy sable mantle vs enwrap,
From feare of perrill and foule horror free.
Let no false treason seeke vs to entrap,
Nor any dread disquiet once annoy
The safety of our ioy:
But let the night be calme and quietsome,
Without tempestuous storms or sad afray:
Lyke as when Ioue with fayre Alcmena lay,
When he begot the great Tirynthian groome:
Or lyke as when he with thy selfe did lie,

121

And begot Maiesty.
And let the mayds and yongmen cease to sing:
Ne let the woods them answer, nor theyr eccho ring.

Let no lamenting cryes, nor dolefull teares,
Be heard all night within nor yet without:
Ne let false whispers, breeding hidden feares,
Breake gentle sleepe with misconceiued dout.
Let no deluding dreames, nor dreadful sights
Make sudden sad affrights;
Ne let housefyres, nor lightnings helplesse harmes,
Ne let the Pouke, nor other euill sprights,
Ne let mischiuous witches with theyr charmes,
Ne let hob Goblins, names whose sence we see not,
Fray vs with things that be not.
Let not the shriech Oule, nor the Storke be heard:
Nor the night Rauen that still deadly yels,
Nor damned ghosts cald vp with mighty spels,
Nor griesly vultures make vs once affeard:
Ne let th'unpleasant Quyre of Frogs still croking
Make vs to wish theyr choking.
Let none of these theyr drery accents sing;
Ne let the woods them answer, nor theyr eccho ring.

Bvt let still Silence trew night watches keepe,
That sacred peace may in assurance rayne,
And tymely sleep, when it is tyme to sleepe,
May poure his limbs forth on your pleasant playne,
The whiles an hundred little winged loues,

Like diuers fethered doues,
Shall fly and flutter round about your bed,
And in the secret darke, that none reproues,
Their prety stealthes shal worke, and snares shal
    spread
To filch away sweet snatches of delight,
Conceald through couert night.
Ye sonnes of Venus, play your sports at will,
For greedy pleasure, carelesse of your toyes,
Thinks more vpon her paradise of ioyes,
Then what ye do, albe it good or ill.
All night therefore attend your merry play,
For it will soone be day:
Now none doth hinder you, that say or sing,
Ne will the woods now answer, nor your Eccho ring.

Who is the same, which at my window peepes?
Or whose is that faire face, that shines so bright,
Is it not Cinthia, she that neuer sleepes,
But walkes about high heauen al the night?
O fayrest goddesse, do thou not enuy
My loue with me to spy:
For thou likewise didst loue, though now vnthought,
And for a fleece of woll, which priuily,
The Latmian shephard once vnto thee brought,
His pleasures with thee wrought.
Therefore to vs be fauorable now;
And sith of wemens labours thou hast charge,
And generation goodly dost enlarge,

Encline thy will t'effect our wishfull vow,
And the chast wombe informe with timely seed,
That may our comfort breed:
Till which we cease our hopefull hap to sing,
Ne let the woods vs answere, nor our Eccho ring.

And thou great Iuno, which with awful might
The lawes of wedlock still dost patronize,
And the religion of the faith first plight
With sacred rites hast taught to solemnize:
And eeke for comfort often called art
Of women in their smart,
Eternally bind thou this louely band,
And all thy blessings vnto vs impart.
And thou glad Genius, in whose gentle hand,
The bridale bowre and geniall bed remaine,
Without blemish or staine,
And the sweet pleasures of theyr loues delight
With secret ayde doest succour and supply,
Till they bring forth the fruitfull progeny,
Send vs the timely fruit of this same night.
And thou fayre Hebe, and thou Hymen free,
Grant that it may so be.
Til which we cease your further prayse to sing,
Ne any woods shal answer, nor your Eccho ring.

And ye high heauens, the temple of the gods,
In which a thousand torches flaming bright
Doe burne, that to vs wretched earthly clods,

In dreadful darknesse lend desired light;
And all ye powers which in the same remayne,
More then we men can fayne,
Poure out your blessing on vs plentiously,
And happy influence vpon vs raine,
That we may raise a large posterity,
Which from the earth, which they may long possesse,
With lasting happinesse,
Vp to your haughty pallaces may mount,
And for the guerdon of theyr glorious merit
May heauenly tabernacles there inherit,
Of blessed Saints for to increase the count.
So let vs rest, sweet loue, in hope of this,
And cease till then our tymely ioyes to sing,
The woods no more vs answer, nor our eccho ring.

Song made in lieu of many ornaments,
With which my loue should duly haue bene dect,
Which cutting off through hasty accidents,
Ye would not stay your dew time to expect,
But promist both to recompens,
Be vnto her a goodly ornament,
And for short time an endlesse moniment.

AN HYMNE OF HEAVENLY BEAVTIE

Rapt with the rage of mine own rauisht thought,
Through contemplation of those goodly sights,
And glorious images in heauen wrought,
Whose wondrous beauty breathing sweet delights,
Do kindle loue in high conceipted sprights:
I faine to tell the things that I behold,
But feele my wits to faile, and tongue to fold.

Vouchsafe then, O thou most almightie Spright,
From whom all guifts of wit and knowledge flow,
To shed into my breast some sparkling light
Of thine eternall Truth, that I may show
Some litle beames to mortall eyes below,
Of that immortall beautie, there with thee,
Which in my weake distraughted mynd I see.

That with the glorie of so goodly sight,
The hearts of men, which fondly here admyre
Faire seeming shewes, and feed on vaine delight,
Transported with celestiall desyre
Of those faire formes, may lift themselues vp hyer,
And learne to loue with zealous humble dewty
Th'eternall fountaine of that heauenly beauty.

Beginning then below, with th'easie vew
Of this base world, subiect to fleshly eye,
From thence to mount aloft by order dew,
To contemplation of th'immortall sky,
Of the soare faulcon so I learne to fly,
That flags awhile her fluttering wings beneath,
Till she her selfe for stronger flight can breath.

Then looke who list, thy gazefull eyes to feed
With sight of that is faire, looke on the frame
Of this wyde *vniuerse*, and therein reed
The endlesse kinds of creatures, which by name
Thou canst not count, much lesse their natures aime:
All which are made with wondrous wise respect,
And all with admirable beautie deckt.

First th'Earth, on adamantine pillers founded,
Amid the Sea engirt with brasen bands;
Then th'Aire still flitting, but yet firmely bounded
On euerie side, with pyles of flaming brands,
Neuer consum'd nor quencht with mortall hands;
And last, that mightie shining christall wall,
Wherewith he hath encompassed this All.

By view whereof, it plainly may appeare,
That still as euery thing doth vpward tend,
And further is from earth, so still more cleare
And faire it growes, till to his perfect end
Of purest beautie, it at last ascend:
Ayre more then water, fire much more then ayre,
And heauen then fire appeares more pure and fayre.

Looke thou no further, but affixe thine eye
On that bright shynie round still mouing Masse,
The house of blessed Gods, which men call *Skye*,
All sowd with glistring stars more thicke then grasse,
Whereof each other doth in brightnesse passe;
But those two most, which ruling night and day,
As King and Queene, the heauens Empire sway.

And tell me then what hast thou euer seene,
That to their beautie may compared bee,
Or can the sight that is most sharpe and keene,
Endure their Captains flaming head to see?
How much lesse those, much higher in degree,
And so much fairer, and much more then these,
As these are fairer then the land and seas?

For farre aboue these heauens which here we see,
Be others farre exceeding these in light,
Not bounded, not corrupt, as these same bee,
But infinite in largenesse and in hight,
Vnmouing, vncorrupt, and spotlesse bright,
That need no Sunne t'illuminate their spheres,
But their owne natiue light farre passing theirs.

And as these heauens still by degrees arize,
Vntill they come to their first Mouers bound,
That in his mightie compasse doth comprize,
And carrie all the rest with him around,
So those likewise doe by degrees redound,
And rise more faire, till they at last ariue
To the most faire, whereto they all do striue.

Faire is the heauen, where happy soules haue place,
In full enioyment of felicitie,
Whence they doe still behold the glorious face
Of the diuine eternall Maiestie;
More faire is that, where those *Idees* on hie,
Enraunged be, which *Plato* so admyred,
And pure *Intelligences* from God inspyred.

Yet fairer is that heauen, in which doe raine
The soueraine *Powres* and mightie *Potentates*,
Which in their high protections doe containe
All mortall Princes, and imperiall States;
And fayrer yet, whereas the royall Seates
And heauenly *Dominations* are set,
From whom all earthly gouernance is fet.

Yet farre more faire be those bright *Cherubins*,
Which all with golden wings are ouerdight,
And those eternall burning *Seraphins*,
Which from their faces dart out fierie light;
Yet fairer then they both, and much more bright
Be th'Angels and Archangels, which attend
On Gods owne person, without rest or end.

These thus in faire each other farre excelling,
As to the Highest they approch more neare,
Yet is that Highest farre beyond all telling,
Fairer then all the rest which there appeare,
Though all their beauties ioynd together were:
How then can mortall tongue hope to expresse,
The image of such endlesse perfectnesse?

Cease then my tongue, and lend vnto my mynd
Leaue to bethinke how great that beautie is,
Whose vtmost parts so beautifull I fynd:
How much more those essentiall parts of his,
His truth, his loue, his wisedome, and his blis,
His grace, his doome, his mercy and his might,
By which he lends vs of himselfe a sight.

Those vnto all he daily doth display,
And shew himselfe in th'image of his grace,
As in a looking glasse, through which he may
Be seene, of all his creatures vile and base,
That are vnable else to see his face,
His glorious face which glistereth else so bright,
That th'Angels selues can not endure his sight.

But we fraile wights, whose sight cannot sustaine
The Suns bright beames, when he on vs doth shyne,
But that their points rebutted backe againe
Are duld, how can we see with feeble eyne,
The glory of that Maiestie diuine,
In sight of whom both Sun and Moone are darke,
Compared to his least resplendent sparke?

The meanes therefore which vnto vs is lent,
Him to behold, is on his workes to looke,
Which he hath made in beauty excellent,
And in the same, as in a brasen booke,
To reade enregistred in euery nooke
His goodnesse, which his beautie doth declare
For all thats good, is beautifull and faire.

Thence gathering plumes of perfect speculation,
To impe the wings of thy high flying mynd,
Mount vp aloft through heauenly contemplation,
From this darke world, whose damps the soule do
    blynd,
And like the natiue brood of Eagles kynd,
On that bright Sunne of glorie fixe thine eyes,
Clear'd from grosse mists of fraile infirmities.

Humbled with feare and awfull reuerence,
Before the footestoole of his Maiestie,
Throw thy selfe downe with trembling innocence,
Ne dare looke vp with corruptible eye
On the dred face of that great *Deity*,
For feare, lest if he chaunce to looke on thee,
Thou turne to nought, and quite confounded be.

But lowly fall before his mercie seate,
Close couered with the Lambes integrity,
From the iust wrath of his auengefull threate,
That sits vpon the righteous throne on hy:
His throne is built vpon Eternity,
More firme and durable then steele or brasse,
Or the hard diamond, which them both doth passe.

His scepter is the rod of Righteousnesse,
With which he bruseth all his foes to dust,
And the great Dragon strongly doth represse,
Vnder the rigour of his iudgement iust;
His seate is Truth, to which the faithfull trust;
From whence proceed her beames so pure and bright,
That all about him sheddeth glorious light.

Light farre exceeding that bright blazing sparke,
Which darted is from *Titans* flaming head,
That with his beames enlumineth the darke
And dampish aire, wherby al things are red:
Whose nature yet so much is maruelled
Of mortall wits, that it doth much amaze
The greatest wisards, which thereon do gaze.

But that immortall light which there doth shine,
Is many thousand times more bright, more cleare,
More excellent, more glorious, more diuine,
Through which to God all mortall actions here,
And euen the thoughts of men, do plaine appeare
For from th'eternall Truth it doth proceed,
Through heauenly vertue, which her beames doe breed.

With the great glorie of that wondrous light,
His throne is all encompassed around,
And hid in his owne brightnesse from the sight
Of all that looke thereon with eyes vnsound:
And vnderneath his feet are to be found
Thunder, and lightning, and tempestuous fyre,
The instruments of his auenging yre.

There in his bosome *Sapience* doth sit,
The soueraine dearling of the *Diety*,
Clad like a Queene in royall robes, most fit
For so great powre and peerelesse maiesty.
And all with gemmes and iewels gorgeously
Adornd, that brighter then the starres appeare,
And make her natiue brightnes seem more cleare.

And on her head a crowne of purest gold
Is set, in signe of highest soueraignty,
And in her hand a scepter she doth hold,
With which she rules the house of God on hy,
And menageth the euer-mouing sky,
And in the same these lower creatures all,
Subiected to her powre imperiall.

Both heauen and earth obey vnto her will,
And all the creatures which they both containe:
For of her fulnesse which the world doth fill,
They all partake, and do in state remaine,
As their great Maker did at first ordaine,
Through obseruation of her high beheast,
By which they first were made, and still increast.

The fairenesse of her face no tongue can tell,
For she the daughters of all wemens race,
And Angels eke, in beautie doth excell,
Sparkled on her from Gods owne glorious face,
And more increast by her owne goodly grace,
That it doth farre exceed all humane thought,
Ne can on earth compared be to ought.

Ne could that Painter (had he liued yet)
Which pictured *Venus* with so curious quill,
That all posteritie admyred it,
Haue purtrayd this, for all his maistring skill;
Ne she her selfe, had she remained still,
And were as faire, as fabling wits do fayne,
Could once come neare this beauty souerayne.

But had those wits the wonders of their dayes
Or that sweete *Teian* Poet which did spend
His plenteous vaine in setting forth her prayse,
Seene but a glims of this, which I pretend,
How wondrously would he her face commend,
Aboue that Idole of his fayning thought,
That all the world should with his rimes be fraught?

How then dare I, the nouice of his Art,
Presume to picture so diuine a wight,
Or hope t'expresse her least perfections part,
Whose beautie filles the heauens with her light,
And darkes the earth with shadow of her sight?
Ah gentle Muse thou art too weake and faint,
The pourtraict of so heauenly hew to paint.

Let Angels which her goodly face behold
And see at will, her soueraigne praises sing,
And those most sacred mysteries vnfold,
Of that faire loue of mightie heauens king.
Enough is me t'admyre so heauenly thing,
And being thus with her huge loue possest,
In th'only wonder of her selfe to rest.

But who so may, thrise happie man him hold,
Of all on earth, whom God so much doth grace,
And lets his owne Beloued to behold:
For in the view of her celestiall face,
All ioy, all blisse, all happinesse haue place,
Ne ought on earth can want vnto the wight,
Who of her selfe can win the wishfull sight.

For she out of her secret threasury,
Plentie of riches forth on him will powre,
Euen heauenly riches, which there hidden ly
Within the closet of her chastest bowre,
Th'eternall portion of her precious dowre,
Which mighty God hath giuen to her free,
And to all those which thereof worthy bee.

None thereof worthy be, but those whom shee
Vouchsafeth to her presence to receaue,
And letteth them her louely face to see,
Whereof such wondrous pleasures they conceaue,
And sweete contentment, that it doth bereaue
Their soule of sense, through infinite delight,
And them transport from flesh into the spright.

In which they see such admirable things,
As carries them into an extasy,
And heare such heauenly notes, and carolings,
Of Gods high praise, that filles the brasen sky,
And feele such ioy and pleasure inwardly,
That maketh them all worldly cares forget,
And onely thinke on that before them set.

Ne from thenceforth doth any fleshly sense,
Or idle thought of earthly things remaine:
But all that earst seemd sweet, seems now offense,
And all that pleased earst, now seemes to paine.
Their ioy, their comfort, their desire, their gaine,
Is fixed all on that which now they see,
All other sights but fayned shadowes bee.

And that faire lampe, which vseth to enflame
The hearts of men with selfe consuming fyre,
Thenceforth seemes fowle, and full of sinfull blame;
And all that pompe, to which proud minds aspyre
By name of honor, and so much desyre,
Seemes to them basenesse, and all riches drosse,
And all mirth sadnesse, and all lucre losse.

So full their eyes are of that glorious sight,
And senses fraught with such satietie,
That in nought else on earth they can delight,
But in th'aspect of that felicitie,
Which they haue written in their inward ey;
On which they feed, and in their fastened mynd
All happie ioy and full contentment fynd.

Ah then my hungry soule, which long hast fed
On idle fancies of thy foolish thought,
And with false beauties flattring bait misled,
Hast after vaine deceiptfull shadowes sought,
Which all are fled, and now haue left thee nought,
But late repentance through thy follies prief;
Ah ceasse to gaze on matter of thy grief.

And looke at last vp to that soueraine light,
From whose pure beams al perfect beauty springs,
That kindleth loue in euery godly spright,
Euen the loue of God, which loathing brings
Of this vile world, and these gay seeming things;
With whose sweete pleasures being so possest,
Thy straying thoughts henceforth for euer rest.

AN EPITAPH UPON THE RIGHT HONOURABLE SIR
PHILLIP SIDNEY

To praise thy life, or waile thy worthie death,
And want thy wit, thy wit high, pure, diuine,
Is far beyond the powre of mortall line,
Nor any one hath worth that draweth breath.

Yet rich in zeale, though poore in learnings lore,
And friendly care obscurde in secret brest,
And loue that enuie in thy life supprest,
Thy deere life done, and death, hath doubled more.

And I, that in thy time and liuing state,
Did onely praise thy vertues in my thought,
As one that seeld the rising sun hath sought,
With words and teares now waile thy timelesse fate.

Drawne was thy race, aright from princely line,
Nor lesse than such, (by gifts that nature gaue,
The common mother that all creatures haue,)
Doth vertue shew and princely linage shine.

A king gaue thee thy name a kingly minde,
That God thee gaue, who found it now too deere
For this base world, and hath resumde it neere,
To sit in skies, and sort with powres diuine.

Kent thy birth daies, and Oxford held thy youth,

The heauens made hast, and staied nor yeers, nor
 time,
The fruits of age grew ripe in thy first prime,
Thy will, thy words: thy words the seales of truth.

Great gifts and wisedom rare imployd thee thence,
To treat from kings, with those more great than kings,
Such hope men had to lay the highest things,
On thy wise youth, to be transported hence.

Whence to sharpe wars sweet honor did thee call,
Thy countries loue, religion, and thy friends
Of worthy men, the marks, the liues and ends,
And her defence, for whom we labor all.

There didst thou vanquish shame and tedious age,
Griefe, sorrow, sicknes, and base fortunes might:
Thy rising day, saw neuer wofull night,
But past with praise, from of this worldly stage.

Back to the campe, by thee that day was brought,
First thine owne death, and after thy long fame;
Teares to the soldiers, the proud Castilians shame;
Vertue exprest, and honor truly taught.

What hath he lost, that such great grace hath woon,
Yoong yeeres, for endles yeeres, and hope vnsure
Of fortunes gifts, for wealth that still shall dure,
Oh happie race with so great praises run.

England doth hold thy lims that bred the same,
Flaunders thy valure where it last was tried,
The Campe thy sorrow where thy bodie died,
Thy friends, thy want; the world, thy vertues fame.

Nations thy wit, our mindes lay vp thy loue,
Letters thy learning, thy losse, yeeres long to come,
In worthy harts sorrow hath made thy tombe,
Thy soule and spright enrich the heauens aboue.

Thy liberall hart imbalmd in gratefull teares,
Yoong sighs, sweet sighes, sage sighes, bewaile thy fall,
Enuie her sting, and spite hath left her gall,
Malice her selfe, a mourning garment weares.

That day their *Hanniball* died, our *Scipio* fell,
Scipio, *Cicero*, and *Petrarch* of our time,
Whose vertues wounded by my worthlesse rime,
Let Angels speake, and heauen thy praises tell.